100+ PYTHON
CODING
CHALLENGES FOR
BEGINNERS

SYNTAX NOMAD

Introduction

Why Learn Python Through Challenges?

Learning Python through challenges is one of the most effective ways to develop problem-solving skills and deepen your understanding of programming concepts. Rather than just reading theory or watching tutorials, solving real problems forces you to think critically and apply what you've learned. Challenges help you:

- **Build Practical Skills:** Coding challenges mimic real-world scenarios where you need to solve problems, often with specific constraints. This prepares you for tasks in jobs, projects, or personal programming endeavors.
- **Develop Logical Thinking:** By working through different levels of problems, you train your mind to break down complex tasks into smaller, manageable pieces, which is essential for any programmer.
- **Stay Engaged:** Challenges make learning interactive and fun. Completing a problem successfully gives a sense of accomplishment that motivates you to keep going.
- **Improve Debugging Abilities:** As you tackle challenges, you'll inevitably run into errors. Fixing these issues helps you develop patience and become familiar with troubleshooting techniques.
- **Prepare for Interviews:** Many coding interviews involve problem-solving exercises. Practicing

challenges equips you with the skills and confidence needed to excel in these settings.

- **Solidify Core Concepts:** Challenges cover topics like loops, conditionals, functions, and data structures, helping you master the basics before moving to more advanced topics.

How to Use This Book

This book is designed to guide you through learning Python step by step, using a challenge-based approach. Here's how you can get the most out of it:

1. **Start with the Basics:** If you're new to Python, begin with the early sections that introduce fundamental concepts like syntax, variables, and basic operations. These sections include simple challenges to help you practice.
2. **Follow a Logical Progression:** The book is structured to gradually increase in difficulty. Start with the beginner-level challenges and move to intermediate ones as you grow more confident.
3. **Solve Before Peeking at Solutions:** Try solving each challenge on your own before referring to the solution. Even if you get stuck, struggling a bit is part of the learning process.
4. **Experiment with Code:** Once you've solved a challenge, try tweaking the code. Change inputs, modify logic, or optimize your solution.

Table of Contents

Experimentation is a great way to deepen your understanding.

5. **Learn from Mistakes:** Don't get discouraged by errors. Use them as learning opportunities to refine your skills. The detailed solutions section provides clear explanations to help you understand where you might have gone wrong.

6. **Take Notes:** Keep a notebook or digital file where you jot down key takeaways, useful functions, or tips you discover while solving problems.

7. **Practice Regularly:** Consistency is key to learning programming. Aim to solve a few challenges every day or week, depending on your schedule.

8. **Use Additional Resources:** If you're struggling with a concept, refer to the resources section at the end of the book or look up explanations online to supplement your understanding.

9. **Review and Revisit:** As you progress, revisit earlier challenges to see how much you've improved or to try alternative solutions.

Apply Your Knowledge: Once you've completed the challenges, use your skills to start working on small projects or contributing to open-source projects. This will help you see how challenges translate to real-world programming tasks. **Tools and Setup for Coding Challenges**

To start solving Python coding challenges, you'll need a few tools and a proper setup. Here's a quick guide to get you started:

1. **Python Installation**
   - Download and install Python from the **official Python website**. Make sure you download the latest version compatible with your operating system.
   - Verify the installation by typing python --version (or python3 --version on some systems) in your command line.
2. **Code Editor or IDE**
   - Choose a code editor or Integrated Development Environment (IDE) that suits your preferences:
     - **VS Code:** Lightweight and highly customizable.
     - **PyCharm:** Feature-rich, ideal for Python development.
     - **IDLE:** Comes pre-installed with Python, great for beginners.
     - **Jupyter Notebook:** Useful for practicing and visualizing output interactively.
3. **Command Line or Terminal**
   - Learn basic command-line operations, as you'll need to run scripts and manage files. On most systems:
     - Windows: Use Command Prompt or PowerShell.
     - macOS/Linux: Use Terminal.
4. **Python Libraries**

o Some challenges may require libraries like math, random, or datetime. These come pre-installed with Python.

o For additional libraries, use pip to install them. For example:

Copy code
pip install library_name

5. **Online Platforms for Quick Practice**
    o Websites like **Replit** or Google Colab let you write and execute Python code in your browser without any installation.

6. **Version Control (Optional for Advanced Practice)**
    o Use Git and GitHub to track your progress or share your solutions. This is particularly useful for more advanced learners who want to maintain a coding portfolio.

7. **Helpful Tools**
    o **Debugger:** Learn to use the debugger in your chosen IDE to identify and fix issues in your code.
    o **Linters:** Tools like flake8 or pylint help catch syntax errors and improve code readability.

Tips for Beginners to Approach Coding Problems

When you're just starting out, tackling coding problems can feel overwhelming. Here's a simple roadmap to make the process manageable and enjoyable:

1. **Understand the Problem**
   - Read the problem statement carefully.
   - Identify the inputs, outputs, and any specific requirements or constraints.
   - Restate the problem in your own words to make sure you understand it.

2. **Break it Down**
   - Divide the problem into smaller parts or steps. For example, if you're solving a math problem, think about how to calculate, format, and print the result in separate steps.
   - Write out these steps in plain language or as comments in your code.

3. **Start Simple**
   - Don't overcomplicate your first solution. Focus on making it work before optimizing.
   - Use simple inputs to test your logic before trying complex scenarios.

4. **Write Pseudocode**
   - Before jumping into actual coding, sketch out a rough plan using pseudocode. This helps you focus on the logic without worrying about syntax.

5. **Test Incrementally**
   - Write and test small parts of the code one step at a time. Debugging smaller sections is much easier than debugging an entire program.

6. **Learn Common Patterns**
   - Familiarize yourself with common problem-solving techniques, such as:
     - Iterating through lists.
     - Using conditional statements.
     - Employing loops for repetitive tasks.
7. **Google and Documentation Are Your Friends**
   - Don't hesitate to look up Python syntax or examples. Use resources like the official Python documentation or forums like Stack Overflow.
8. **Handle Errors Gracefully**
   - If your code doesn't work as expected, don't panic. Start by reading the error message to understand what went wrong.
   - Use print statements or a debugger to trace the flow of your code.
9. **Focus on Learning, Not Perfection**
   - Your initial solutions might not be the most efficient or elegant, and that's okay. With practice, you'll improve over time.
10. **Practice Regularly**
    - Consistency is key. Set aside dedicated time each day or week to solve coding problems, even if it's just 10–15 minutes.
11. **Review Solutions**
    - Once you've solved a problem, review your solution and compare it to others. This helps you find better or alternative approaches.
12. **Celebrate Small Wins**

○ Every solved problem, no matter how simple, is progress. Take pride in completing challenges and use them as motivation to tackle harder ones.

Getting Started: Basic Syntax and Operations

Printing Output

Printing output in Python is one of the first steps in learning the language. It allows you to display results, messages, or debug information. Python uses the print() function for this purpose.

- **Basic Syntax**:

  python
  Copy code
  ```python
  print("Hello, World!")
  print(42)
  print("The result is:", 5 + 3)
  ```

- **Formatting Output**: Use f-strings (available from Python 3.6) to format strings easily:

  python
  Copy code
  ```python
  name = "Alice"
  age = 25
  print(f"My name is {name} and I am {age} years old.")
  ```

- **Escape Sequences**: Special characters can be included in strings using escape sequences:

  python
  Copy code

```python
print("Hello\nWorld!")  # Newline
print("He said, \"Python is great!\"")  # Quotation
marks
```

- **Multiple Arguments**: The print() function can handle multiple arguments, separated by commas:

```python
Copy code
print("The sum of", 3, "and", 5, "is", 3 + 5)
```

Basic Arithmetic Operations

Python supports basic arithmetic operations that are easy to use. Here are the primary operators:

- **Addition** (+):

```python
Copy code
result = 3 + 5
print(result)  # Output: 8
```

- **Subtraction** (-):

```python
Copy code
result = 10 - 4
print(result)  # Output: 6
```

- **Multiplication** (*):

```python
Copy code
result = 6 * 7
print(result)  # Output: 42
```

- **Division (/):**

```python
Copy code
result = 15 / 3
print(result)  # Output: 5.0
```

- **Integer Division (//):** Returns the quotient without the decimal part.

```python
Copy code
result = 15 // 4
print(result)  # Output: 3
```

- **Modulo (%):** Returns the remainder of division.

```python
Copy code
result = 15 % 4
print(result)  # Output: 3
```

- **Exponentiation (**):** Raises a number to a power.

```python
Copy code
result = 2 ** 3
```

```python
print(result)  # Output: 8
```

- **Order of Operations**: Python follows the standard mathematical order (PEMDAS):

```python
Copy code
result = 2 + 3 * 4
print(result)  # Output: 14 (multiplication first)
```

Variables and Data Types

Variables are used to store data that can be used and manipulated later in your code. Python automatically determines the data type based on the value assigned.

- **Declaring Variables**:

```python
Copy code
x = 10
name = "John"
is_happy = True
```

- **Common Data Types**:
  - **Integer (int)**: Whole numbers.

    ```python
    Copy code
    age = 30
    ```

  - **Float (float)**: Numbers with decimal points.

```python
Copy code
temperature = 36.5
```

- **String (str)**: Text.

```python
Copy code
greeting = "Hello, Python!"
```

- **Boolean (bool)**: True or False values.

```python
Copy code
is_active = False
```

- **Type Checking**: Use the type() function to check the type of a variable.

```python
Copy code
print(type(10))       # Output: <class 'int'>
print(type(3.14))     # Output: <class 'float'>
print(type("Python")) # Output: <class 'str'>
print(type(True))     # Output: <class 'bool'>
```

- **Type Conversion**: Convert between data types when needed.

```python
Copy code
x = 5     # int
```

```python
y = str(x)  # Convert to string
z = float(x)  # Convert to float
print(y, z)  # Output: '5', 5.0
```

Taking User Input

Python allows you to take input from users using the input() function. The input is always returned as a string, so you may need to convert it into other data types for numerical operations.

- **Basic Usage**:

python
Copy code
```python
name = input("What is your name? ")
print(f"Hello, {name}!")
```

- **Converting Input**: Use functions like int() or float() to convert the input into numeric types.

python
Copy code
```python
age = int(input("How old are you? "))
print(f"You will be {age + 1} next year.")
```

- **Example with Multiple Inputs**:

python
Copy code
```python
a = int(input("Enter the first number: "))
b = int(input("Enter the second number: "))
```

```python
print(f"The sum of {a} and {b} is {a + b}.")
```

Challenge Set 1: Hello World Variations

These challenges focus on practicing the basics of output formatting and variations of the classic "Hello, World!" program.

1. **Challenge 1: Basic Hello World**
   - Write a program that prints "Hello, World!".

   Example:

   ```python
   python
   Copy code
   print("Hello, World!")
   ```

2. **Challenge 2: Personalized Greeting**
   - Ask the user for their name and print a personalized greeting.

   Example:

   ```python
   python
   Copy code
   name = input("Enter your name: ")
   print(f"Hello, {name}!")
   ```

3. **Challenge 3: Multi-line Message**

- ○ Print a greeting message on multiple lines using escape sequences.

   Example:

   python
   Copy code
   print("Hello,\nWorld!\nWelcome to Python.")

4. **Challenge 4: Custom Separator**
   - ○ Print "Hello" and "World" separated by a custom character (e.g., -).

   Example:

   python
   Copy code
   print("Hello", "World", sep="-")

5. **Challenge 5: Emoji Greeting**
   - ○ Print "Hello, World!" with an emoji included.

   Example:

   python
   Copy code
   print("Hello, World! ☺")

Challenge Set 2: Simple Calculations (Sum, Difference, Product)

These challenges help you practice arithmetic operations using user input.

1. **Challenge 1: Add Two Numbers**
   - Write a program that takes two numbers from the user and prints their sum.

   Example:

   ```python
   Copy code
   a = int(input("Enter the first number: "))
   b = int(input("Enter the second number: "))
   print(f"The sum is: {a + b}")
   ```

2. **Challenge 2: Subtract Two Numbers**
   - Ask the user for two numbers and calculate their difference.

   Example:

   ```python
   Copy code
   a = int(input("Enter the first number: "))
   b = int(input("Enter the second number: "))
   print(f"The difference is: {a - b}")
   ```

3. **Challenge 3: Multiply Two Numbers**
   - Write a program that multiplies two numbers provided by the user.

Example:

```python
Copy code
a = int(input("Enter the first number: "))
b = int(input("Enter the second number: "))
print(f"The product is: {a * b}")
```

4. **Challenge 4: Simple Calculator**
   - Create a simple calculator that performs addition, subtraction, multiplication, and division based on the user's choice.

Example:

```python
Copy code
a = float(input("Enter the first number: "))
b = float(input("Enter the second number: "))
operation = input("Choose an operation (+, -, *, /): ")

if operation == "+":
    print(f"The sum is: {a + b}")
elif operation == "-":
    print(f"The difference is: {a - b}")
elif operation == "*":
    print(f"The product is: {a * b}")
elif operation == "/":
    print(f"The quotient is: {a / b}")
else:
```

```
    print("Invalid operation")
```

5. **Challenge 5: Square of a Number**
   - Ask the user for a number and calculate its square.

Example:

python
Copy code
```
num = int(input("Enter a number: "))
print(f"The square of {num} is {num ** 2}.")
```

Control Flow Basics

If-Else Statements

If-else statements are the backbone of decision-making in Python. They allow the program to execute different blocks of code based on specific conditions.

- **Basic Syntax**:

```python
Copy code
if condition:
    # Code to execute if condition is True
else:
    # Code to execute if condition is False
```

- **Example**:

```python
Copy code
age = int(input("Enter your age: "))
if age >= 18:
    print("You are an adult.")
else:
    print("You are a minor.")
```

- **Using Elif for Multiple Conditions**: The elif statement is used for checking multiple conditions.

```python
Copy code
```

```python
marks = int(input("Enter your marks: "))
if marks >= 90:
    print("Grade: A")
elif marks >= 75:
    print("Grade: B")
elif marks >= 50:
    print("Grade: C")
else:
    print("Grade: F")
```

Nested Conditionals

Nested conditionals are if-else statements placed inside another if-else block. They are useful when the decision depends on multiple layers of conditions.

- **Syntax**:

```python
Copy code
if condition1:
    if condition2:
        # Code to execute if both conditions are True
    else:
        # Code to execute if condition1 is True but condition2 is False
else:
    # Code to execute if condition1 is False
```

- **Example**:

```python
Copy code
age = int(input("Enter your age: "))
if age >= 18:
    citizenship = input("Are you a citizen? (yes/no): ").lower()
    if citizenship == "yes":
        print("You are eligible to vote.")
    else:
        print("You must be a citizen to vote.")
else:
    print("You are not old enough to vote.")
```

- **Avoiding Over-Nesting**: Overusing nested conditionals can make code harder to read. Use logical operators or restructure conditions to simplify.

Logical Operators (and, or, not)

Logical operators are used to combine multiple conditions or negate conditions.

- **and**: Returns True if all conditions are True.

```python
Copy code
age = int(input("Enter your age: "))
has_id = input("Do you have an ID? (yes/no): ").lower() == "yes"
if age >= 18 and has_id:
```

```python
    print("You can enter.")
else:
    print("Access denied.")
```

- **or**: Returns True if at least one condition is True.

```python
python
Copy code
weather = input("Is it sunny or warm? (yes/no): ").lower()
if weather == "yes":
    print("You can go for a walk.")
else:
    print("Stay indoors.")
```

- **not**: Negates the condition.

```python
python
Copy code
is_raining = input("Is it raining? (yes/no): ").lower() == "yes"
if not is_raining:
    print("You can go outside without an umbrella.")
else:
    print("Take an umbrella with you.")
```

- **Combining Logical Operators**: Logical operators can be combined for more complex conditions.

```python
python
Copy code
age = int(input("Enter your age: "))
```

```python
has_ticket = input("Do you have a ticket? (yes/no): ").lower() == "yes"
if age >= 18 and (has_ticket or age == 17):
    print("You are allowed to enter.")
else:
    print("Entry not allowed.")
```

Challenge Set 3: Number Comparisons

These challenges will help you practice decision-making using comparison and logical operators.

1. **Challenge 1: Larger of Two Numbers**
   - Write a program that asks the user for two numbers and prints the larger one.

   Example:

   python
   Copy code
   ```python
   a = int(input("Enter the first number: "))
   b = int(input("Enter the second number: "))
   if a > b:
       print(f"The larger number is {a}.")
   else:
       print(f"The larger number is {b}.")
   ```

2. **Challenge 2: Check Positive, Negative, or Zero**
   - Ask the user for a number and print whether it is positive, negative, or zero.

Example:

```python
num = int(input("Enter a number: "))
if num > 0:
    print("The number is positive.")
elif num < 0:
    print("The number is negative.")
else:
    print("The number is zero.")
```

3. **Challenge 3: Compare Three Numbers**
   - Write a program that asks for three numbers and prints the largest one.

Example:

```python
a = int(input("Enter the first number: "))
b = int(input("Enter the second number: "))
c = int(input("Enter the third number: "))
if a >= b and a >= c:
    print(f"The largest number is {a}.")
elif b >= a and b >= c:
    print(f"The largest number is {b}.")
else:
    print(f"The largest number is {c}.")
```

4. **Challenge 4: Even or Odd**

o   Ask the user for a number and determine if it
    is even or odd.

Example:

python
Copy code
num = int(input("Enter a number: "))
if num % 2 == 0:
    print("The number is even.")
else:
    print("The number is odd.")

Challenge Set 4: Grade Calculator

These challenges focus on using conditional statements to
calculate and assign grades.

1. **Challenge 1: Single Grade**
    o   Write a program that asks the user for their
        score (0–100) and assigns a grade:
        ▪   A: 90–100
        ▪   B: 80–89
        ▪   C: 70–79
        ▪   D: 60–69
        ▪   F: Below 60

Example:

python
Copy code
score = int(input("Enter your score (0-100): "))

```python
if score >= 90:
    print("Grade: A")
elif score >= 80:
    print("Grade: B")
elif score >= 70:
    print("Grade: C")
elif score >= 60:
    print("Grade: D")
else:
    print("Grade: F")
```

2. **Challenge 2: Grade Validation**
   - o Modify the program to check if the score is valid (0–100). If not, print an error message.

Example:

python
Copy code
```python
score = int(input("Enter your score (0-100): "))
if 0 <= score <= 100:
    if score >= 90:
        print("Grade: A")
    elif score >= 80:
        print("Grade: B")
    elif score >= 70:
        print("Grade: C")
```

```python
    elif score >= 60:
        print("Grade: D")
    else:
        print("Grade: F")
else:
    print("Error: Invalid score.")
```

3. **Challenge 3: Average Grade**
   - Ask the user for three test scores, calculate the average, and assign a grade based on the average.

   Example:

   python
   Copy code
```python
test1 = int(input("Enter score for Test 1: "))
test2 = int(input("Enter score for Test 2: "))
test3 = int(input("Enter score for Test 3: "))
average = (test1 + test2 + test3) / 3

if average >= 90:
    print("Grade: A")
elif average >= 80:
    print("Grade: B")
elif average >= 70:
    print("Grade: C")
elif average >= 60:
    print("Grade: D")
else:
    print("Grade: F")
```

Challenge Set 5: Leap Year Checker

These challenges help you practice nested conditionals and modulus operations.

1. **Challenge 1: Basic Leap Year Check**
   o Write a program to check if a given year is a leap year. A leap year:
      ▪ Is divisible by 4.
      ▪ But not divisible by 100 unless also divisible by 400.

   Example:

   ```python
   Copy code
   year = int(input("Enter a year: "))
   if year % 4 == 0:
       if year % 100 == 0:
           if year % 400 == 0:
               print(f"{year} is a leap year.")
           else:
               print(f"{year} is not a leap year.")
       else:
           print(f"{year} is a leap year.")
   else:
       print(f"{year} is not a leap year.")
   ```

2. **Challenge 2: Optimized Leap Year Check**
   o Simplify the conditions using logical operators.

Example:

```python
Copy code
year = int(input("Enter a year: "))
if (year % 4 == 0 and year % 100 != 0) or (year % 400 == 0):
    print(f"{year} is a leap year.")
else:
    print(f"{year} is not a leap year.")
```

3. **Challenge 3: Leap Year for a Range**
   - Write a program to check and print all leap years in a given range of years.

Example:

```python
Copy code
start_year = int(input("Enter the start year: "))
end_year = int(input("Enter the end year: "))
for year in range(start_year, end_year + 1):
    if (year % 4 == 0 and year % 100 != 0) or (year % 400 == 0):
        print(year)
```

Loops: For and While

Using For Loops

For loops in Python are used to iterate over a sequence, such as a list, range, string, or dictionary.

- **Basic Syntax**:

```python
Copy code
for item in sequence:
    # Code to execute for each item
```

- **Example: Iterating Over a List**:

```python
Copy code
numbers = [1, 2, 3, 4]
for num in numbers:
    print(num)
```

- **Using range()**: The range() function generates a sequence of numbers.

```python
Copy code
for i in range(5):
    print(i)  # Output: 0, 1, 2, 3, 4
```

- **Looping Through a String**:

```python
```

```
Copy code
word = "Python"
for letter in word:
    print(letter)
```

While Loops Basics

While loops are used when the number of iterations is not known in advance. They continue until a specific condition is false.

- **Basic Syntax**:

```python
Copy code
while condition:
    # Code to execute
```

- **Example: Countdown**:

```python
Copy code
count = 5
while count > 0:
    print(count)
    count -= 1
```

- **Infinite Loops**: Be cautious of infinite loops where the condition never becomes false.

```python
```

```
Copy code
while True:
    print("This will run forever!")
```

- **Example with User Input**:

```python
Copy code
password = ""
while password != "secret":
    password = input("Enter the password: ")
print("Access granted!")
```

Break and Continue Statements

- **break**: Exits the loop immediately when a condition is met.

```python
Copy code
for i in range(10):
    if i == 5:
        break
    print(i)  # Stops printing when i == 5
```

- **continue**: Skips the current iteration and moves to the next one.

```python
Copy code
for i in range(10):
```

```python
    if i % 2 == 0:
        continue
    print(i)  # Prints only odd numbers
```

- **Using break in a While Loop**:

```python
python
Copy code
while True:
    num = int(input("Enter a number (0 to stop): "))
    if num == 0:
        break
    print(f"You entered {num}.")
```

- **Using continue in a While Loop**:

```python
python
Copy code
count = 0
while count < 10:
    count += 1
    if count % 2 == 0:
        continue
    print(count)  # Prints only odd numbers
```

Challenge Set 6: Multiplication Tables

These challenges use loops to generate multiplication tables.

1. **Challenge 1: Single Table**

- Write a program that generates the multiplication table for a number provided by the user.

Example:

```python
Copy code
num = int(input("Enter a number: "))
for i in range(1, 11):
    print(f"{num} x {i} = {num * i}")
```

2. **Challenge 2: All Tables from 1 to 10**
   - Create a program that prints the multiplication tables for numbers from 1 to 10.

Example:

```python
Copy code
for num in range(1, 11):
    print(f"Multiplication Table for {num}")
    for i in range(1, 11):
        print(f"{num} x {i} = {num * i}")
    print()  # Blank line between tables
```

3. **Challenge 3: Reverse Multiplication Table**
   - Print a multiplication table in reverse order (e.g., 10 down to 1).

Example:

```python
Copy code
num = int(input("Enter a number: "))
for i in range(10, 0, -1):
    print(f"{num} x {i} = {num * i}")
```

4. **Challenge 4: Skip Multiples of a Number**
   - Generate a multiplication table but skip multiples of 5.

Example:

```python
Copy code
num = int(input("Enter a number: "))
for i in range(1, 11):
    if (num * i) % 5 == 0:
        continue
    print(f"{num} x {i} = {num * i}")
```

5. **Challenge 5: Custom Range Multiplication Table**
   - Allow the user to specify the range for the multiplication table (e.g., start and end values).

Example:

```python
Copy code
num = int(input("Enter a number: "))
```

```python
start = int(input("Enter the start of the range: "))
end = int(input("Enter the end of the range: "))
for i in range(start, end + 1):
    print(f"{num} x {i} = {num * i}")
```

Challenge Set 7: Fibonacci Sequence Generator

These challenges focus on generating Fibonacci sequences using loops and user input.

1. **Challenge 1: Generate a Fixed Number of Fibonacci Terms**
   - Write a program to generate the first n terms of the Fibonacci sequence, where n is provided by the user.

   Example:

   python
   Copy code
   ```python
   n = int(input("Enter the number of terms: "))
   a, b = 0, 1
   for _ in range(n):
       print(a, end=" ")
       a, b = b, a + b
   ```

2. **Challenge 2: Fibonacci Sequence Below a Certain Value**
   - Generate all Fibonacci numbers less than a user-defined maximum value.

Example:

```python
Copy code
max_value = int(input("Enter the maximum value: "))
a, b = 0, 1
while a < max_value:
    print(a, end=" ")
    a, b = b, a + b
```

3. **Challenge 3: Check if a Number is in the Fibonacci Sequence**
   - Ask the user for a number and determine if it is part of the Fibonacci sequence.

Example:

```python
Copy code
num = int(input("Enter a number: "))
a, b = 0, 1
found = False
while a <= num:
    if a == num:
        found = True
        break
    a, b = b, a + b
if found:
    print(f"{num} is in the Fibonacci sequence.")
else:
```

```python
print(f"{num} is not in the Fibonacci sequence.")
```

4. **Challenge 4: Reverse Fibonacci**
   - o Generate a Fibonacci sequence in reverse order, starting from the nth term.

Example:

```python
python
Copy code
n = int(input("Enter the number of terms: "))
fib = [0, 1]
for _ in range(2, n):
    fib.append(fib[-1] + fib[-2])
for num in reversed(fib):
    print(num, end=" ")
```

5. **Challenge 5: Fibonacci Series with User-defined Starting Numbers**
   - o Allow the user to input two starting numbers for a custom Fibonacci sequence.

Example:

```python
python
Copy code
a = int(input("Enter the first number: "))
b = int(input("Enter the second number: "))
n = int(input("Enter the number of terms: "))
for _ in range(n):
```

```python
    print(a, end=" ")
    a, b = b, a + b
```

Challenge Set 8: Countdown Timer

These challenges focus on creating timers using loops, incorporating user input and delays.

1. **Challenge 1: Basic Countdown**
   - Create a countdown timer that starts from a user-defined number and prints each number down to 0.

   Example:

   ```python
   python
   Copy code
   import time

   n = int(input("Enter the starting number for the countdown: "))
   for i in range(n, -1, -1):
       print(i)
       time.sleep(1)  # Pause for 1 second between
   numbers
   print("Time's up!")
   ```

2. **Challenge 2: Custom Interval Countdown**
   - Allow the user to specify the interval between numbers in the countdown.

Example:

```python
import time

n = int(input("Enter the starting number for the countdown: "))
interval = float(input("Enter the time interval in seconds: "))
for i in range(n, -1, -1):
    print(i)
    time.sleep(interval)
print("Done!")
```

3. **Challenge 3: Countdown with Warnings**
   - Display a warning message when the countdown reaches specific points, like 5 seconds remaining.

   Example:

```python
import time

n = int(input("Enter the starting number for the countdown: "))
for i in range(n, -1, -1):
    if i == 5:
        print("Warning: Only 5 seconds left!")
```

```
    print(i)
    time.sleep(1)
print("Boom!")
```

4. **Challenge 4: Countdown with Beeping Sounds**
   - Add sound effects (beep or bell) at the end of the countdown.

   Example (for systems with terminal bell sound):

   python
   Copy code
   ```python
   import time

   n = int(input("Enter the starting number for the countdown: "))
   for i in range(n, -1, -1):
       print(i)
       time.sleep(1)
   print("\a")  # Produces a beep sound
   print("Timer finished!")
   ```

5. **Challenge 5: Countdown with Progress Bar**
   - Create a visual progress bar that updates as the countdown progresses.

   Example:

   python
   Copy code
   ```python
   import time
   ```

```python
n = int(input("Enter the countdown time in seconds: "))
for i in range(n, -1, -1):
    progress = "#" * (n - i) + "-" * i
    print(f"[{progress}] {i} seconds remaining", end="\r")
    time.sleep(1)
print("\nCountdown complete!")
```

Working with Strings

String Basics and Methods

Strings in Python are sequences of characters enclosed in quotes, either single (') or double (").

- **Creating Strings**:

```python
Copy code
single_quote_string = 'Hello'
double_quote_string = "World"
multiline_string = """This is
a multiline
string."""
```

- **String Properties**:
    - Strings are immutable, meaning they cannot be changed after creation.
    - Strings are iterable, so you can loop through them character by character.
- **Common String Methods**:

```python
Copy code
text = "hello world"

# Changing case
print(text.upper())    # Output: "HELLO WORLD"
print(text.lower())    # Output: "hello world"
print(text.capitalize())  # Output: "Hello world"
```

```python
print(text.title())   # Output: "Hello World"

# Finding and replacing
print(text.find("world"))  # Output: 6
print(text.replace("world", "Python"))  # Output:
"hello Python"

# Splitting and joining
words = text.split()  # Splits by spaces by default
print(words)  # Output: ['hello', 'world']
print(" ".join(words))  # Joins words with spaces

# Checking content
print(text.startswith("hello"))  # Output: True
print(text.endswith("Python"))  # Output: False
print(text.isalpha())  # False (contains spaces)
print("hello".isalpha())  # True
print("123".isdigit())  # True
```

Slicing and Indexing

Python strings can be accessed and manipulated using indexing and slicing.

- **Indexing**:
    - Access individual characters using square brackets ([]).
    - Indexing starts at 0 (left to right) and -1 (right to left).

```python
Copy code
text = "Python"
print(text[0])  # Output: 'P' (first character)
print(text[-1])  # Output: 'n' (last character)
```

- **Slicing**:
    - Extract portions of a string using the [start:end:step] syntax.
    - The end index is exclusive.

```python
Copy code
text = "Python"
print(text[0:3])  # Output: 'Pyt' (characters from index 0 to 2)
print(text[:3])  # Output: 'Pyt' (start defaults to 0)
print(text[3:])  # Output: 'hon' (end defaults to the end of the string)
print(text[::2])  # Output: 'Pto' (every second character)
print(text[::-1])  # Output: 'nohtyP' (reversed string)
```

- **Modifying Strings Using Slicing**: While strings are immutable, you can create new strings by combining slices.

```python
Copy code
text = "Pthon"
text = text[:1] + "y" + text[2:]
```

```python
print(text)  # Output: "Python"
```

String Formatting

String formatting allows you to create dynamic strings by inserting variables or expressions into placeholders.

- **Using f-Strings** (Recommended for Python 3.6+):

```python
Copy code
name = "Alice"
age = 25
print(f"My name is {name} and I am {age} years old.")
```

- **Using .format()**:

```python
Copy code
print("My name is {} and I am {} years old.".format(name, age))
print("The sum of {0} and {1} is {2}.".format(3, 5, 3 + 5))  # Positional arguments
print("Name: {name}, Age: {age}".format(name=name, age=age))  # Named arguments
```

- **Old-Style Formatting** (Not Recommended for New Projects):

```python
```

```
Copy code
print("My name is %s and I am %d years old." %
(name, age))
```

- **Formatting Numbers**:

```python
Copy code
pi = 3.14159
print(f"Pi rounded to 2 decimal places: {pi:.2f}")  #
Output: "3.14"
print("Pi rounded to 3 decimal places:
{:.3f}".format(pi))  # Output: "3.142"
```

- **Padding and Alignment**:

```python
Copy code
text = "Python"
print(f"{text:>10}")  # Right-align (output: '
Python')
print(f"{text:<10}")  # Left-align (output: 'Python
')
print(f"{text:^10}")  # Center-align (output: '
Python  ')
```
Challenge Set 9: Palindrome Checker

A palindrome is a word, phrase, or number that reads the
same backward as forward.

1. **Challenge 1: Check if a Word is a Palindrome**
   - Write a program that asks the user for a word and checks if it is a palindrome.

   Example:

   python
   Copy code
   ```
   word = input("Enter a word: ").lower()
   if word == word[::-1]:
       print(f"'{word}' is a palindrome.")
   else:
       print(f"'{word}' is not a palindrome.")
   ```

2. **Challenge 2: Ignore Spaces and Case Sensitivity**
   - Modify the program to ignore spaces and capitalization when checking for palindromes.

   Example:

   python
   Copy code
   ```
   text = input("Enter a phrase: ").lower().replace(" ",
   "")
   if text == text[::-1]:
       print("It's a palindrome!")
   else:
       print("It's not a palindrome.")
   ```

3. **Challenge 3: Sentence-Level Palindrome**

o Extend the program to handle punctuation (e.g., "A man, a plan, a canal: Panama").

Example:

```python
python
Copy code
import string
text = input("Enter a sentence: ").lower()
cleaned_text = "".join(char for char in text if char.isalnum())
if cleaned_text == cleaned_text[::-1]:
    print("It's a palindrome!")
else:
    print("It's not a palindrome.")
```

Challenge Set 10: Word Counter

This set focuses on counting words and characters in text.

1. **Challenge 1: Count Words in a Sentence**
   o Write a program that counts the number of words in a sentence provided by the user.

   Example:

   ```python
   python
   Copy code
   sentence = input("Enter a sentence: ")
   words = sentence.split()
   print(f"The sentence contains {len(words)} words.")
   ```

2. **Challenge 2: Count Specific Words**

- o Modify the program to count the occurrences of a specific word.

Example:

```python
Copy code
sentence = input("Enter a sentence: ").lower()
word_to_count = input("Enter the word to count: ").lower()
word_count = sentence.split().count(word_to_count)
print(f"The word '{word_to_count}' appears {word_count} times.")
```

3. **Challenge 3: Count Characters**
   - o Write a program to count the total number of characters in a sentence, excluding spaces.

Example:

```python
Copy code
sentence = input("Enter a sentence: ")
char_count = len(sentence.replace(" ", ""))
print(f"The sentence contains {char_count} characters (excluding spaces).")
```

4. **Challenge 4: Frequency of Each Word**
   - o Create a program that displays the frequency of each word in a sentence.

Example:

```python
Copy code
sentence = input("Enter a sentence: ").lower()
words = sentence.split()
word_frequency = {}
for word in words:
    word_frequency[word] =
word_frequency.get(word, 0) + 1
print("Word frequencies:")
for word, count in word_frequency.items():
    print(f"{word}: {count}")
```

Challenge Set 11: Pig Latin Converter

Pig Latin is a fun transformation of English words. Rules:

- For words that start with a vowel, add "yay" to the end (e.g., "apple" → "appleyay").
- For words that start with a consonant, move the first consonant cluster to the end and add "ay" (e.g., "hello" → "ellohay").

1. **Challenge 1: Convert a Single Word**
   - Write a program to convert a single word to Pig Latin.

   Example:

   ```python
   Copy code
   word = input("Enter a word: ").lower()
   ```

```python
vowels = "aeiou"
if word[0] in vowels:
    pig_latin = word + "yay"
else:
    for i, char in enumerate(word):
        if char in vowels:
            pig_latin = word[i:] + word[:i] + "ay"
            break
print(f"Pig Latin: {pig_latin}")
```

2. **Challenge 2: Handle Multiple Words**
   o Extend the program to convert an entire sentence to Pig Latin.

Example:

```python
Copy code
sentence = input("Enter a sentence: ").lower()
vowels = "aeiou"
words = sentence.split()
pig_latin_words = []
for word in words:
    if word[0] in vowels:
        pig_latin_words.append(word + "yay")
    else:
        for i, char in enumerate(word):
            if char in vowels:
                pig_latin_words.append(word[i:] + word[:i] + "ay")
                break
```

```python
pig_latin_sentence = " ".join(pig_latin_words)
print(f"Pig Latin: {pig_latin_sentence}")
```

3. **Challenge 3: Handle Punctuation**
   o Modify the program to preserve punctuation when converting sentences to Pig Latin.

Example:

```python
python
Copy code
import string

sentence = input("Enter a sentence: ").lower()
vowels = "aeiou"
words = sentence.split()
pig_latin_words = []

for word in words:
    stripped_word = word.strip(string.punctuation)
    prefix = "".join(c for c in word if c in
string.punctuation)
    suffix = "".join(c for c in reversed(word) if c in
string.punctuation)

    if stripped_word[0] in vowels:
        pig_latin = stripped_word + "yay"
    else:
        for i, char in enumerate(stripped_word):
            if char in vowels:
```

```python
            pig_latin = stripped_word[i:] +
stripped_word[:i] + "ay"
                break
    pig_latin_words.append(prefix + pig_latin +
suffix)

pig_latin_sentence = " ".join(pig_latin_words)
print(f"Pig Latin: {pig_latin_sentence}")
```

Lists and Tuples

List Basics and Operations

Lists are ordered, mutable collections that can hold items of any data type. They are one of the most versatile data structures in Python.

- **Creating a List**:

  python
  Copy code
  ```python
  empty_list = []  # Empty list
  numbers = [1, 2, 3, 4, 5]  # List of integers
  mixed_list = [1, "hello", 3.5, True]  # List with mixed data types
  ```

- **Accessing Elements**:
    - Use indexing to access items.
    - Indexing starts from 0 (left-to-right) and -1 (right-to-left).

  python
  Copy code
  ```python
  numbers = [10, 20, 30, 40]
  print(numbers[0])  # Output: 10
  print(numbers[-1])  # Output: 40
  ```

- **Modifying Elements**: Lists are mutable, so you can change their elements.

  python

```
Copy code
numbers[1] = 25
print(numbers)  # Output: [10, 25, 30, 40]
```

- **Adding Elements**:
  - Append an element to the end:

    ```python
    Copy code
    numbers.append(50)
    print(numbers)  # Output: [10, 25, 30, 40, 50]
    ```

  - Insert an element at a specific position:

    ```python
    Copy code
    numbers.insert(2, 35)
    print(numbers)  # Output: [10, 25, 35, 30, 40, 50]
    ```

- **Removing Elements**:
  - Remove by value:

    ```python
    Copy code
    numbers.remove(25)
    print(numbers)  # Output: [10, 35, 30, 40, 50]
    ```

  - Remove by index:

    ```python
    Copy code
    ```

```python
del numbers[1]
print(numbers)  # Output: [10, 30, 40, 50]
```

- Pop the last element (or a specific index):

```python
python
Copy code
last = numbers.pop()
print(last)  # Output: 50
print(numbers)  # Output: [10, 30, 40]
```

- **List Slicing**:

```python
python
Copy code
sublist = numbers[1:3]
print(sublist)  # Output: [30, 40]
```

- **List Concatenation and Repetition**:

```python
python
Copy code
list1 = [1, 2]
list2 = [3, 4]
combined = list1 + list2
print(combined)  # Output: [1, 2, 3, 4]

repeated = list1 * 3
print(repeated)  # Output: [1, 2, 1, 2, 1, 2]
```

Using Tuples

Tuples are similar to lists but are immutable, meaning their contents cannot be changed after creation.

- **Creating Tuples**:

```python
Copy code
empty_tuple = ()  # Empty tuple
single_element = (1,)  # Single element (comma required)
numbers = (10, 20, 30)  # Tuple of integers
mixed_tuple = (1, "hello", 3.5, True)  # Tuple with mixed data types
```

- **Accessing Elements**: Tuples use indexing like lists.

```python
Copy code
print(numbers[0])  # Output: 10
print(numbers[-1])  # Output: 30
```

- **Tuple Unpacking**: Assign tuple elements to variables.

```python
Copy code
a, b, c = numbers
print(a, b, c)  # Output: 10 20 30
```

- **Immutability**: Once a tuple is created, its elements cannot be modified.

```python
Copy code
numbers[0] = 5  # Error: 'tuple' object does not
support item assignment
```

- **Converting Between Lists and Tuples**:
  - Convert a tuple to a list:

    ```python
    Copy code
    numbers_list = list(numbers)
    print(numbers_list)  # Output: [10, 20, 30]
    ```

  - Convert a list to a tuple:

    ```python
    Copy code
    numbers_tuple = tuple(numbers_list)
    print(numbers_tuple)  # Output: (10, 20, 30)
    ```

Common Methods for Lists

Python lists have several built-in methods for various operations.

- **Add Elements**:
  - append(): Add a single element to the end.
  - extend(): Add multiple elements from another iterable.

    ```python
    Copy code
    numbers = [1, 2]
    ```

```python
numbers.extend([3, 4])
print(numbers)  # Output: [1, 2, 3, 4]
```

- **Remove Elements**:
  - remove(value): Remove the first occurrence of a value.
  - pop(index): Remove and return the element at the given index (default is the last element).
  - clear(): Remove all elements.

```python
Copy code
numbers.clear()
print(numbers)  # Output: []
```

- **Sorting and Reversing**:
  - sort(): Sort the list in ascending order (in-place).

```python
Copy code
numbers = [4, 2, 3, 1]
numbers.sort()
print(numbers)  # Output: [1, 2, 3, 4]
```

  - reverse(): Reverse the order of the list.

```python
Copy code
numbers.reverse()
print(numbers)  # Output: [4, 3, 2, 1]
```

- o sorted(): Return a new sorted list without modifying the original.

```python
Copy code
numbers = [4, 2, 3, 1]
print(sorted(numbers))  # Output: [1, 2, 3, 4]
```

- **Finding Values**:
  - o index(value): Return the index of the first occurrence of a value.
  - o count(value): Count how many times a value appears in the list.

```python
Copy code
numbers = [1, 2, 3, 2, 4]
print(numbers.count(2))  # Output: 2
```

- **Copying a List**:
  - o Use copy() to create a shallow copy.

```python
Copy code
copy_numbers = numbers.copy()
print(copy_numbers)  # Output: [1, 2, 3, 4]
```

- **Membership Tests**: Use the in keyword to check for existence.

```python
Copy code
```

```
print(3 in numbers)  # Output: True
print(5 in numbers)  # Output: False
```
Challenge Set 12: Sum and Average of a List

1. **Challenge 1: Sum of a List**
   o Write a program to calculate the sum of all numbers in a list.

   Example:

   ```python
   Copy code
   numbers = [10, 20, 30, 40, 50]
   total = sum(numbers)
   print(f"The sum of the list is: {total}")
   ```

2. **Challenge 2: Average of a List**
   o Write a program to calculate the average of numbers in a list.

   Example:

   ```python
   Copy code
   numbers = [10, 20, 30, 40, 50]
   total = sum(numbers)
   average = total / len(numbers)
   print(f"The average of the list is: {average}")
   ```

3. **Challenge 3: Exclude Non-Numeric Values**

- Extend the program to handle lists containing non-numeric values. Ignore them while calculating the sum and average.

Example:

python
Copy code
```
items = [10, "hello", 20, 30, None, 40]
valid_numbers = [x for x in items if isinstance(x, (int, float))]
total = sum(valid_numbers)
average = total / len(valid_numbers)
print(f"The sum is: {total}, and the average is: {average}")
```
Challenge Set 13: Find Maximum and Minimum

1. **Challenge 1: Find the Maximum**
   - Write a program to find the largest number in a list.

Example:

python
Copy code
```
numbers = [10, 20, 30, 40, 50]
max_value = max(numbers)
print(f"The maximum value in the list is: {max_value}")
```

2. **Challenge 2: Find the Minimum**

- o Write a program to find the smallest number in a list.

Example:

```python
Copy code
numbers = [10, 20, 30, 40, 50]
min_value = min(numbers)
print(f"The minimum value in the list is: {min_value}")
```

3. **Challenge 3: Without Using Built-in Functions**
   - o Write a program to find the maximum and minimum values in a list without using max() or min().

Example:

```python
Copy code
numbers = [10, 20, 30, 40, 50]
max_value = numbers[0]
min_value = numbers[0]
for num in numbers:
    if num > max_value:
        max_value = num
    if num < min_value:
        min_value = num
print(f"Maximum: {max_value}, Minimum: {min_value}")
```

4. **Challenge 4: Handle Mixed Data**
   - o Extend the program to handle lists containing non-numeric values, ignoring them while finding the maximum and minimum.

   Example:

   ```python
   python
   Copy code
   items = [10, "hello", 20, 30, None, 40]
   valid_numbers = [x for x in items if isinstance(x, (int, float))]
   max_value = max(valid_numbers)
   min_value = min(valid_numbers)
   print(f"Maximum: {max_value}, Minimum: {min_value}")
   ```

Challenge Set 14: Rotate a List

1. **Challenge 1: Rotate Right by 1**
   - o Write a program to rotate a list to the right by 1 position.

   Example:

   ```python
   python
   Copy code
   numbers = [1, 2, 3, 4, 5]
   rotated = [numbers[-1]] + numbers[:-1]
   print(f"Rotated list: {rotated}")
   ```

2. **Challenge 2: Rotate Left by 1**

- o Write a program to rotate a list to the left by 1 position.

Example:

python
Copy code
numbers = [1, 2, 3, 4, 5]
rotated = numbers[1:] + [numbers[0]]
print(f"Rotated list: {rotated}")

3. **Challenge 3: Rotate by N Positions**
   - o Allow the user to specify the number of positions to rotate the list. Handle both left and right rotations.

Example:

python
Copy code
numbers = [1, 2, 3, 4, 5]
n = int(input("Enter the number of positions to rotate: "))
direction = input("Enter direction (left/right): ").lower()

if direction == "right":
    rotated = numbers[-n:] + numbers[:-n]
elif direction == "left":
    rotated = numbers[n:] + numbers[:n]
else:

```python
    print("Invalid direction")
    rotated = numbers

print(f"Rotated list: {rotated}")
```

4. **Challenge 4: Handle Large Rotations**
   o Modify the program to handle cases where the number of positions exceeds the length of the list.

   Example:

```python
python
Copy code
numbers = [1, 2, 3, 4, 5]
n = int(input("Enter the number of positions to rotate: "))
direction = input("Enter direction (left/right): ").lower()
n = n % len(numbers)  # Reduce rotations to within list length

if direction == "right":
    rotated = numbers[-n:] + numbers[:-n]
elif direction == "left":
    rotated = numbers[n:] + numbers[:n]
else:
    print("Invalid direction")
    rotated = numbers

print(f"Rotated list: {rotated}")
```

5. Challenge 5: Circular List Rotation

  o Implement a program to perform infinite
     rotations on a list until the user decides to
     stop.

Example:

```python
Copy code
numbers = [1, 2, 3, 4, 5]
while True:
    direction = input("Enter direction (left/right or 'stop' to exit): ").lower()
    if direction == "stop":
        break
    elif direction == "right":
        numbers = numbers[-1:] + numbers[:-1]
    elif direction == "left":
        numbers = numbers[1:] + numbers[:1]
    else:
        print("Invalid direction")
        continue
    print(f"Current list: {numbers}")
```

Dictionaries

Basics of Dictionaries

Dictionaries in Python are unordered collections of key-value pairs. They allow for efficient data retrieval based on unique keys.

- **Creating a Dictionary**:

```python
Copy code
empty_dict = {}  # An empty dictionary
person = {
    "name": "Alice",
    "age": 25,
    "city": "New York"
}
```

- **Key Characteristics**:
  - Keys must be unique and immutable (e.g., strings, numbers, tuples).
  - Values can be of any data type and can be duplicated.
- **Accessing Dictionary Keys and Values**:

```python
Copy code
print(person["name"])  # Output: Alice
print(person.get("age"))  # Output: 25
print(person.get("gender", "Not specified"))  # Default if key is missing
```

- **Checking for Keys**:

```python
Copy code
print("age" in person)  # Output: True
print("gender" in person)  # Output: False
```

Accessing and Modifying Values

- **Accessing Values**: Use square brackets ([]) or the .get() method to access values.

```python
Copy code
person = {"name": "Alice", "age": 25, "city": "New York"}
print(person["name"])  # Output: Alice
print(person.get("city"))  # Output: New York
```

- **Adding New Key-Value Pairs**:

```python
Copy code
person["gender"] = "Female"
print(person)  # Output: {'name': 'Alice', 'age': 25, 'city': 'New York', 'gender': 'Female'}
```

- **Updating Existing Values**:

```python
Copy code
```

```python
person["age"] = 26
print(person)  # Output: {'name': 'Alice', 'age': 26, 'city': 'New York'}
```

- **Removing Key-Value Pairs**:
    - Using del:

        python
        Copy code
        ```python
        del person["city"]
        print(person)  # Output: {'name': 'Alice', 'age': 25}
        ```

    - Using .pop():

        python
        Copy code
        ```python
        age = person.pop("age")
        print(age)  # Output: 25
        print(person)  # Output: {'name': 'Alice'}
        ```

    - Using .popitem() to remove the last inserted item (Python 3.7+):

        python
        Copy code
        ```python
        item = person.popitem()
        print(item)  # Output: ('name', 'Alice')
        ```

- **Clearing the Dictionary**:

    python

```
Copy code
person.clear()
print(person)  # Output: {}
```
Iterating Through Dictionaries

You can iterate over dictionaries to access keys, values, or both.

- **Iterating Through Keys**:

```python
Copy code
person = {"name": "Alice", "age": 25, "city": "New York"}
for key in person:
    print(key)
# Output:
# name
# age
# city
```

- **Iterating Through Values**:

```python
Copy code
for value in person.values():
    print(value)
# Output:
# Alice
# 25
# New York
```

- **Iterating Through Key-Value Pairs**: Use .items() to retrieve both keys and values in the loop.

```python
Copy code
for key, value in person.items():
    print(f"{key}: {value}")
# Output:
# name: Alice
# age: 25
# city: New York
```

- **Counting Items in a Dictionary**:

```python
Copy code
print(len(person))  # Output: 3
```

- **Iterating in a Sorted Order (By Keys)**:

```python
Copy code
for key in sorted(person):
    print(f"{key}: {person[key]}")
# Output:
# age: 25
# city: New York
# name: Alice
```

Challenge Set 15: Frequency Counter

These challenges focus on counting occurrences of elements using dictionaries.

1. **Challenge 1: Count Character Frequency**
   - o Write a program to count the frequency of each character in a string.

   Example:

   ```python
   Copy code
   text = input("Enter a string: ").lower()
   frequency = {}
   for char in text:
       if char.isalnum():  # Consider only alphanumeric characters
           frequency[char] = frequency.get(char, 0) + 1
   print("Character Frequency:")
   for char, count in frequency.items():
       print(f"{char}: {count}")
   ```

2. **Challenge 2: Count Word Frequency**
   - o Write a program to count the frequency of each word in a sentence.

   Example:

   ```python
   Copy code
   sentence = input("Enter a sentence: ").lower()
   words = sentence.split()
   word_frequency = {}
   for word in words:
   ```

```python
        word_frequency[word] =
word_frequency.get(word, 0) + 1
print("Word Frequency:")
for word, count in word_frequency.items():
    print(f"{word}: {count}")
```

3. **Challenge 3: Most Frequent Character**
   - Modify the character frequency program to identify the most frequently occurring character.

   Example:

   ```python
   python
   Copy code
   text = input("Enter a string: ").lower()
   frequency = {}
   for char in text:
       if char.isalnum():
           frequency[char] = frequency.get(char, 0) + 1
   most_frequent = max(frequency,
   key=frequency.get)
   print(f"The most frequent character is
   '{most_frequent}' with a count of
   {frequency[most_frequent]}.")
   ```

Challenge Set 16: Simple Phonebook

Create a program that simulates a basic phonebook using a dictionary.

1. **Challenge 1: Add Contacts**

- Write a program to add contacts to a phonebook.

Example:

```python
Copy code
phonebook = {}
while True:
    name = input("Enter contact name (or 'stop' to finish): ").strip()
    if name.lower() == "stop":
        break
    phone = input(f"Enter phone number for {name}: ").strip()
    phonebook[name] = phone
print("Phonebook:")
for name, phone in phonebook.items():
    print(f"{name}: {phone}")
```

2. **Challenge 2: Search for a Contact**
   - Extend the program to allow users to search for a contact by name.

Example:

```python
Copy code
name_to_search = input("Enter the name to search: ").strip()
```

```python
if name_to_search in phonebook:
    print(f"{name_to_search}:
{phonebook[name_to_search]}")
else:
    print("Contact not found.")
```

3. **Challenge 3: Update or Delete Contacts**
   o Add options to update or delete a contact.

Example:

python
Copy code
```python
option = input("Do you want to update or delete a contact? (update/delete): ").strip().lower()
if option == "update":
    name = input("Enter the name of the contact to update: ").strip()
    if name in phonebook:
        phone = input(f"Enter the new phone number for {name}: ").strip()
        phonebook[name] = phone
        print(f"{name} updated successfully.")
    else:
        print("Contact not found.")
elif option == "delete":
    name = input("Enter the name of the contact to delete: ").strip()
    if name in phonebook:
        del phonebook[name]
        print(f"{name} deleted successfully.")
```

else:
        print("Contact not found.")
Challenge Set 17: Translate Words

These challenges involve using a dictionary to create a simple word translation system.

1. **Challenge 1: Create a Translation Dictionary**
   - ○ Write a program that lets the user input words in one language and their translations in another language.

   Example:

   ```python
   Copy code
   translation_dict = {}
   while True:
       word = input("Enter a word (or 'stop' to finish): ").strip()
       if word.lower() == "stop":
           break
       translation = input(f"Enter the translation for '{word}': ").strip()
       translation_dict[word] = translation
   print("Translation Dictionary:")
   for word, translation in translation_dict.items():
       print(f"{word}: {translation}")
   ```

2. **Challenge 2: Translate a Sentence**

○ Write a program that translates a sentence
using the dictionary.

Example:

python
Copy code
```
sentence = input("Enter a sentence: ").strip()
translated_sentence = []
for word in sentence.split():

translated_sentence.append(translation_dict.get(word, word))  # Keep the word if no translation exists
print("Translated Sentence:", " ".join(translated_sentence))
```

3. **Challenge 3: Handle Missing Words**
   ○ Modify the program to allow the user to add
   missing words to the dictionary during
   translation.

Example:

python
Copy code
```
sentence = input("Enter a sentence: ").strip()
translated_sentence = []
for word in sentence.split():
    if word in translation_dict:

translated_sentence.append(translation_dict[word])
```

```python
    else:
        print(f"No translation for '{word}'.")
        add_translation = input("Do you want to add
it? (yes/no): ").strip().lower()
        if add_translation == "yes":
            translation = input(f"Enter the translation for
'{word}': ").strip()
            translation_dict[word] = translation
            translated_sentence.append(translation)
        else:
            translated_sentence.append(word)
print("Translated Sentence:", "
".join(translated_sentence))
```

4. **Challenge 4: Reverse Lookup**
   - Add functionality to look up words by their translations.

Example:

python
Copy code
```python
translation_to_search = input("Enter the translation
to search for: ").strip()
reverse_dict = {value: key for key, value in
translation_dict.items()}
word = reverse_dict.get(translation_to_search, "No
matching word found")
print(f"Original word: {word}")
```

Functions

Defining Functions

Functions in Python allow you to organize code into reusable blocks. They are defined using the def keyword.

- **Basic Syntax**:

```python
Copy code
def function_name():
    # Code to execute
```

- **Example**:

```python
Copy code
def greet():
    print("Hello, World!")

greet()  # Output: Hello, World!
```

- **Why Use Functions?**
    - **Code Reusability**: Write once, use multiple times.
    - **Organization**: Break complex tasks into smaller, manageable chunks.
    - **Readability**: Easier to understand and maintain.

Function Arguments

Arguments are values passed to a function when it is called. They allow functions to work dynamically based on input.

- **Positional Arguments**:
  - The simplest way to pass data to a function.

python
Copy code
```
def greet(name):
    print(f"Hello, {name}!")

greet("Alice")  # Output: Hello, Alice!
```

- **Default Arguments**:
  - Provide default values if no arguments are passed.

python
Copy code
```
def greet(name="World"):
    print(f"Hello, {name}!")

greet()  # Output: Hello, World!
greet("Alice")  # Output: Hello, Alice!
```

- **Keyword Arguments**:
  - Pass arguments by specifying their names.

python
Copy code
```
def introduce(name, age):
```

```
    print(f"My name is {name} and I am {age} years
old.")

introduce(age=25, name="Alice")  # Output: My
name is Alice and I am 25 years old.
```

- **Variable-Length Arguments**:
  - Use *args for positional arguments and
    **kwargs for keyword arguments.

python
Copy code
```python
def add_numbers(*args):
    print(f"The sum is: {sum(args)}")

add_numbers(1, 2, 3, 4)  # Output: The sum is: 10

def display_info(**kwargs):
    for key, value in kwargs.items():
        print(f"{key}: {value}")

display_info(name="Alice", age=25, city="New
York")
# Output:
# name: Alice
# age: 25
# city: New York
```
Return Values

Functions can return values using the return statement.
This allows the caller to capture and use the result.

- **Returning a Single Value**:

```python
Copy code
def square(number):
    return number ** 2

result = square(5)
print(result)  # Output: 25
```

- **Returning Multiple Values**:
    - Use a tuple to return multiple values.

```python
Copy code
def calculate(a, b):
    return a + b, a - b, a * b, a / b

results = calculate(10, 5)
print(results)  # Output: (15, 5, 50, 2.0)
```

- **Using a Function's Return Value**:
    - Return values can be passed directly to other functions or expressions.

```python
Copy code
def double(number):
    return number * 2

print(double(5) + 10)  # Output: 20
```

Examples Combining Concepts

1. **Simple Calculator**:

python
Copy code
```python
def calculator(a, b, operation="add"):
    if operation == "add":
        return a + b
    elif operation == "subtract":
        return a - b
    elif operation == "multiply":
        return a * b
    elif operation == "divide":
        if b != 0:
            return a / b
        else:
            return "Error: Division by zero"
    else:
        return "Invalid operation"

print(calculator(10, 5, "add"))       # Output: 15
print(calculator(10, 5, "subtract"))  # Output: 5
print(calculator(10, 5, "multiply"))  # Output: 50
print(calculator(10, 0, "divide"))    # Output: Error:
Division by zero
```

2. **Find the Maximum of Three Numbers**:

python
Copy code

```python
def find_max(a, b, c):
    return max(a, b, c)

print(find_max(10, 20, 15))  # Output: 20
```

3. **Greeting Multiple People**:

python
Copy code
```python
def greet_people(*names):
    for name in names:
        print(f"Hello, {name}!")

greet_people("Alice", "Bob", "Charlie")
# Output:
# Hello, Alice!
# Hello, Bob!
# Hello, Charlie!
```

Challenge Set 18: Calculator Function

These challenges involve creating a calculator function that performs various mathematical operations.

1. **Challenge 1: Basic Calculator**
   - Write a function that takes two numbers and an operator (+, -, *, /) and returns the result.

Example:

python
Copy code
```python
def calculator(a, b, operator):
```

```python
    if operator == "+":
        return a + b
    elif operator == "-":
        return a - b
    elif operator == "*":
        return a * b
    elif operator == "/":
        if b != 0:
            return a / b
        else:
            return "Error: Division by zero"
    else:
        return "Invalid operator"

print(calculator(10, 5, "+"))  # Output: 15
print(calculator(10, 0, "/"))  # Output: Error:
Division by zero
```

2. **Challenge 2: Extended Calculator**
   o Add support for more operations like
     modulus (%), exponentiation (**), and floor
     division (//).

Example:

```python
Copy code
def extended_calculator(a, b, operator):
    if operator == "+":
        return a + b
    elif operator == "-":
```

```python
        return a - b
    elif operator == "*":
        return a * b
    elif operator == "/":
        return a / b if b != 0 else "Error: Division by
zero"
    elif operator == "%":
        return a % b
    elif operator == "**":
        return a ** b
    elif operator == "//":
        return a // b
    else:
        return "Invalid operator"

print(extended_calculator(10, 3, "%"))  # Output: 1
print(extended_calculator(2, 3, "**"))  # Output: 8
```

3. **Challenge 3: User Input Calculator**
   - Create a program that takes user input for numbers and the operator, and then calls the calculator function.

Example:

```python
Copy code
def user_calculator():
    a = float(input("Enter the first number: "))
```

```
b = float(input("Enter the second number: "))
operator = input("Enter the operator (+, -, *, /): ")
result = calculator(a, b, operator)
print(f"The result is: {result}")
```

```
user_calculator()
```

Challenge Set 19: Prime Number Checker

These challenges focus on checking whether a number is prime.

1. **Challenge 1: Basic Prime Checker**
   o Write a function that checks if a number is prime.

   Example:

   ```python
   Copy code
   def is_prime(n):
       if n <= 1:
           return False
       for i in range(2, int(n ** 0.5) + 1):
           if n % i == 0:
               return False
       return True

   print(is_prime(7))   # Output: True
   print(is_prime(10))  # Output: False
   ```

2. **Challenge 2: Prime Checker with User Input**

- Create a program that takes a number from the user and determines if it is prime.

Example:

```python
python
Copy code
num = int(input("Enter a number: "))
if is_prime(num):
    print(f"{num} is a prime number.")
else:
    print(f"{num} is not a prime number.")
```

3. **Challenge 3: List of Primes in a Range**
   - Write a function that generates a list of all prime numbers in a given range.

Example:

```python
python
Copy code
def primes_in_range(start, end):
    primes = []
    for num in range(start, end + 1):
        if is_prime(num):
            primes.append(num)
    return primes

print(primes_in_range(10, 50))
# Output: [11, 13, 17, 19, 23, 29, 31, 37, 41, 43, 47]
```

Challenge Set 20: Factorial Calculator

These challenges involve calculating the factorial of a number.

1. **Challenge 1: Basic Factorial**
   - Write a function to calculate the factorial of a number.

   Example:

   ```python
   Copy code
   def factorial(n):
       if n == 0 or n == 1:
           return 1
       else:
           return n * factorial(n - 1)

   print(factorial(5))  # Output: 120
   ```

2. **Challenge 2: Iterative Factorial**
   - Write a non-recursive version of the factorial function.

   Example:

   ```python
   Copy code
   def iterative_factorial(n):
       result = 1
       for i in range(1, n + 1):
           result *= i
       return result
   ```

```
print(iterative_factorial(5))  # Output: 120
```

3. **Challenge 3: Factorial with User Input**
   - Write a program that takes a number from the user and calculates its factorial.

   Example:

   python
   Copy code
   ```
   num = int(input("Enter a number: "))
   print(f"The factorial of {num} is {factorial(num)}")
   ```

4. **Challenge 4: Factorial of a List of Numbers**
   - Write a program to calculate the factorial of every number in a given list.

   Example:

   python
   Copy code
   ```
   numbers = [3, 4, 5]
   factorials = [factorial(n) for n in numbers]
   print(factorials)  # Output: [6, 24, 120]
   ```

Error and Exception Handling

Understanding Errors in Python

Errors in Python are divided into two main categories:

1. **Syntax Errors**:
   - Occur when the code violates Python's syntax rules.
   - These errors are detected before the program runs. **Example**:

   python
   Copy code
   print("Hello" # Missing closing parenthesis

   Output:

   javascript
   Copy code
   SyntaxError: unexpected EOF while parsing

2. **Exceptions**:
   - Occur during runtime when Python encounters something it cannot handle.
   - Examples include:
     - **ZeroDivisionError**: Division by zero.
     - **TypeError**: Using incorrect data types in operations.
     - **NameError**: Using a variable that hasn't been defined.

- **IndexError**: Accessing a list index that doesn't exist. **Example**:

```python
python
Copy code
print(1 / 0)  # Division by zero
```

Output:

```vbnet
vbnet
Copy code
ZeroDivisionError: division by zero
```

Using Try-Except Blocks

The try-except block handles exceptions and prevents the program from crashing.

- **Basic Syntax**:

```python
python
Copy code
try:
    # Code that might cause an error
except ExceptionType:
    # Code to handle the exception
```

- **Example: Catching a Specific Exception**:

```python
python
Copy code
try:
    num = int(input("Enter a number: "))
```

```python
    print(f"10 divided by {num} is {10 / num}")
except ZeroDivisionError:
    print("You can't divide by zero!")
except ValueError:
    print("Invalid input. Please enter a valid number.")
```

- **Catching All Exceptions**: Use except without specifying the exception type, but this is not recommended unless you are debugging.

python
Copy code
```python
try:
    num = int(input("Enter a number: "))
    print(f"10 divided by {num} is {10 / num}")
except:
    print("An error occurred.")
```

- **Using else and finally**:
    o else: Executes if no exception is raised.
    o finally: Executes whether or not an exception is raised.

python
Copy code
```python
try:
    num = int(input("Enter a number: "))
    result = 10 / num
except ZeroDivisionError:
    print("You can't divide by zero!")
```

```python
except ValueError:
    print("Invalid input. Please enter a valid
number.")
else:
    print(f"Result is {result}")
finally:
    print("Execution complete.")
```

Raising Custom Exceptions

You can manually raise exceptions in Python using the raise keyword. This is useful for enforcing specific conditions in your code.

- **Raising Built-in Exceptions**:

```python
python
Copy code
age = int(input("Enter your age: "))
if age < 0:
    raise ValueError("Age cannot be negative.")
print(f"Your age is {age}.")
```

- **Defining Custom Exceptions**:
  - Create a custom exception class by inheriting from the Exception class.

```python
python
Copy code
class NegativeNumberError(Exception):
    pass
```

```python
def calculate_square_root(num):
    if num < 0:
        raise NegativeNumberError("Cannot calculate
the square root of a negative number.")
    return num ** 0.5

try:
    print(calculate_square_root(-4))
except NegativeNumberError as e:
    print(e)
```

- **Using Custom Messages**:

  python
  Copy code
  ```python
  class CustomError(Exception):
      def __init__(self, message):
          self.message = message
          super().__init__(self.message)

  try:
      raise CustomError("This is a custom error
  message.")
  except CustomError as e:
      print(f"Caught an error: {e}")
  ```

Best Practices for Error Handling

1. **Be Specific**: Catch specific exceptions to avoid masking unrelated issues.

   python

```
Copy code
try:
    result = 10 / num
except ZeroDivisionError:
    print("Division by zero is not allowed.")
```

2. **Avoid Bare except**: Using a bare except can catch unexpected errors and make debugging difficult.
3. **Use Finally for Cleanup**: Use the finally block for tasks like closing files or releasing resources.

```python
Copy code
try:
    file = open("data.txt", "r")
except FileNotFoundError:
    print("File not found.")
finally:
    file.close()
```

4. **Validate Inputs**: Prevent exceptions by checking inputs before executing operations.

```python
Copy code
num = input("Enter a number: ")
if not num.isdigit():
    print("Please enter a valid number.")
```

5. **Log Exceptions**: Log errors for debugging and monitoring purposes in production environments.

```python
Copy code
import logging

logging.basicConfig(filename="app.log",
level=logging.ERROR)

try:
    num = 10 / 0
except ZeroDivisionError as e:
    logging.error("An exception occurred: %s", e)
```

Challenge Set 21: Safe Division

These challenges focus on implementing division operations with error handling to ensure the program doesn't crash due to invalid input or division by zero.

1. **Challenge 1: Basic Safe Division**
   - Write a function that safely divides two numbers, catching division by zero errors.

   Example:

```python
Copy code
def safe_division(a, b):
    try:
        return a / b
```

```
        except ZeroDivisionError:
            return "Error: Division by zero is not allowed."

print(safe_division(10, 2))  # Output: 5.0
print(safe_division(10, 0))  # Output: Error:
Division by zero is not allowed.
```

2. **Challenge 2: Safe Division with User Input**
   - ○ Modify the program to accept user input for the numbers.

   Example:

   ```python
   python
   Copy code
   def safe_division():
       try:
           a = float(input("Enter the numerator: "))
           b = float(input("Enter the denominator: "))
           result = a / b
           print(f"The result is: {result}")
       except ZeroDivisionError:
           print("Error: Division by zero is not allowed.")
       except ValueError:
           print("Error: Please enter valid numbers.")

   safe_division()
   ```

3. **Challenge 3: Retry Safe Division**
   - ○ Add a loop that lets the user retry if an error occurs.

Example:

```python
Copy code
def safe_division():
    while True:
        try:
            a = float(input("Enter the numerator: "))
            b = float(input("Enter the denominator: "))
            result = a / b
            print(f"The result is: {result}")
            break
        except ZeroDivisionError:
            print("Error: Division by zero is not allowed. Try again.")
        except ValueError:
            print("Error: Please enter valid numbers.")

safe_division()
```

4. **Challenge 4: Return a Default Value**
   o Modify the function to return a default value if an error occurs.

Example:

```python
Copy code
def safe_division(a, b, default=None):
```

```python
    try:
        return a / b
    except ZeroDivisionError:
        return default

print(safe_division(10, 0, default="Undefined"))  #
Output: Undefined
```

Challenge Set 22: Input Validation

These challenges focus on validating user input to ensure
the program processes only valid data.

1. **Challenge 1: Validate Integer Input**
   o Write a program that ensures the user enters
     an integer.

   Example:

```python
python
Copy code
def get_integer():
    while True:
        try:
            num = int(input("Enter an integer: "))
            return num
        except ValueError:
            print("Error: That's not a valid integer. Try
again.")

number = get_integer()
print(f"You entered: {number}")
```

2. **Challenge 2: Validate Float Input**
   o Modify the program to ensure the user enters a floating-point number.

Example:

```python
Copy code
def get_float():
    while True:
        try:
            num = float(input("Enter a floating-point number: "))
            return num
        except ValueError:
            print("Error: That's not a valid number. Try again.")

number = get_float()
print(f"You entered: {number}")
```

3. **Challenge 3: Validate Input in a Range**
   o Ensure the user enters a number within a specified range.

Example:

```python
Copy code
def get_number_in_range(min_val, max_val):
    while True:
```

```python
    try:
        num = int(input(f"Enter a number between {min_val} and {max_val}: "))
        if min_val <= num <= max_val:
            return num
        else:
            print(f"Error: The number must be between {min_val} and {max_val}.")
    except ValueError:
        print("Error: That's not a valid number. Try again.")

number = get_number_in_range(1, 10)
print(f"You entered: {number}")
```

4. **Challenge 4: Validate Multiple Conditions**
   o Write a program to validate input for multiple conditions (e.g., a positive integer that is even).

Example:

```
python
Copy code
def get_positive_even_number():
    while True:
        try:
            num = int(input("Enter a positive even number: "))
            if num > 0 and num % 2 == 0:
                return num
```

```
        else:
            print("Error: The number must be positive
and even.")
    except ValueError:
        print("Error: That's not a valid number. Try
again.")

number = get_positive_even_number()
print(f"You entered: {number}")
```

5. **Challenge 5: Validate String Input**
   - Ensure the user enters a non-empty string
     with only alphabetic characters.

Example:

```python
Copy code
def get_valid_string():
    while True:
        text = input("Enter a non-empty alphabetic
string: ").strip()
        if text.isalpha():
            return text
        else:
            print("Error: The input must contain only
letters and cannot be empty.")

valid_string = get_valid_string()
print(f"You entered: {valid_string}")
```

6. Challenge 6: Combine Validations

- ○ Write a program that validates multiple inputs at once, such as name, age, and email.

Example:

```python
Copy code
def get_valid_name():
    while True:
        name = input("Enter your name: ").strip()
        if name.isalpha():
            return name
        else:
            print("Error: Name must contain only letters.")

def get_valid_age():
    while True:
        try:
            age = int(input("Enter your age: "))
            if age > 0:
                return age
            else:
                print("Error: Age must be a positive number.")
        except ValueError:
            print("Error: That's not a valid age.")

def get_valid_email():
    while True:
```

```python
    email = input("Enter your email: ").strip()
    if "@" in email and "." in email:
        return email
    else:
        print("Error: Please enter a valid email address.")


name = get_valid_name()
age = get_valid_age()
email = get_valid_email()
print(f"Name: {name}, Age: {age}, Email: {email}")
```

File Handling
Reading and Writing Files

Python provides simple methods to work with files using the open() function.

1. Opening a File

- **Basic Syntax**:

  python
  Copy code
  ```
  file = open("filename.txt", mode)
  ```

  - Modes:
    - 'r': Read mode (default).
    - 'w': Write mode (overwrites the file if it exists).
    - 'a': Append mode (adds content to the end of the file).
    - 'b': Binary mode (used with 'rb', 'wb').

2. Reading Files

- **Read Entire Content**:

  python
  Copy code
  ```
  with open("example.txt", "r") as file:
      content = file.read()
      print(content)
  ```

- **Read Line by Line**:

```python
Copy code
with open("example.txt", "r") as file:
    for line in file:
        print(line.strip())
```

- **Read Specific Number of Characters**:

```python
Copy code
with open("example.txt", "r") as file:
    content = file.read(10)  # Reads the first 10 characters
    print(content)
```

3. Writing to Files

- **Write Content**:

```python
Copy code
with open("example.txt", "w") as file:
    file.write("Hello, World!")
```

- **Append Content**:

```python
Copy code
with open("example.txt", "a") as file:
    file.write("\nThis is an appended line.")
```

4. Closing Files

- Using the with statement automatically closes the file after the block is executed.

File Operations

Python provides useful methods for file handling using the os module.

1. Checking File Existence

python
Copy code
```python
import os
if os.path.exists("example.txt"):
    print("File exists.")
else:
    print("File does not exist.")
```
2. Renaming a File

python
Copy code
```python
os.rename("old_name.txt", "new_name.txt")
```
3. Deleting a File

python
Copy code
```python
os.remove("example.txt")
```
4. Creating a Directory

python

Copy code
```
os.mkdir("new_folder")
```
5. Deleting a Directory

python
Copy code
```
os.rmdir("new_folder")
```
6. Listing Files in a Directory

python
Copy code
```
files = os.listdir(".")
print(files)
```
Working with CSV Files

CSV (Comma-Separated Values) files are commonly used for data storage. Python's csv module simplifies reading and writing CSV files.

1. Reading a CSV File

- **Using csv.reader():**

  python
  Copy code
  ```
  import csv
  ```

```python
with open("data.csv", "r") as file:
    reader = csv.reader(file)
    for row in reader:
        print(row)
```

- **Skipping the Header Row**:

python
Copy code
```python
with open("data.csv", "r") as file:
    reader = csv.reader(file)
    next(reader)  # Skip the header row
    for row in reader:
        print(row)
```

2. Writing to a CSV File

- **Using csv.writer()**:

python
Copy code
```python
with open("output.csv", "w", newline="") as file:
    writer = csv.writer(file)
    writer.writerow(["Name", "Age", "City"])  # Writing header
    writer.writerow(["Alice", 25, "New York"])  # Writing a single row
    writer.writerows([["Bob", 30, "London"], ["Charlie", 35, "Paris"]])  # Writing multiple rows
```

3. Reading and Writing with DictReader and DictWriter

- **Reading as Dictionaries**:

```python
Copy code
with open("data.csv", "r") as file:
    reader = csv.DictReader(file)
    for row in reader:
        print(row["Name"], row["Age"])
```

- **Writing as Dictionaries**:

```python
Copy code
with open("output.csv", "w", newline="") as file:
    fieldnames = ["Name", "Age", "City"]
    writer = csv.DictWriter(file, fieldnames=fieldnames)
    writer.writeheader()  # Writing header
    writer.writerow({"Name": "Alice", "Age": 25, "City": "New York"})  # Writing a single row
    writer.writerows([
        {"Name": "Bob", "Age": 30, "City": "London"},
        {"Name": "Charlie", "Age": 35, "City": "Paris"}
    ])  # Writing multiple rows
```

Example: Combining File and CSV Operations

Task: Merge Multiple CSV Files

- Combine data from multiple CSV files into one.

```python
Copy code
import csv
import os

files = ["file1.csv", "file2.csv", "file3.csv"]
output_file = "merged.csv"

with open(output_file, "w", newline="") as outfile:
    writer = csv.writer(outfile)
    writer.writerow(["Name", "Age", "City"])  # Writing header

    for file in files:
        if os.path.exists(file):
            with open(file, "r") as infile:
                reader = csv.reader(infile)
                next(reader)  # Skip header of each file
                for row in reader:
                    writer.writerow(row)

print(f"Data merged into {output_file}")
```

Challenge Set 23: Line Counter in a File

1. **Challenge 1: Count Total Lines**
   - Write a program to count the number of lines in a text file.

   Example:

```python
Copy code
def count_lines(file_name):
    try:
        with open(file_name, "r") as file:
            return sum(1 for line in file)
    except FileNotFoundError:
        return "Error: File not found."

print(count_lines("example.txt"))
```

2. **Challenge 2: Count Non-Empty Lines**
   - Modify the program to count only non-empty lines.

Example:

```python
Copy code
def count_non_empty_lines(file_name):
    try:
        with open(file_name, "r") as file:
            return sum(1 for line in file if line.strip())
    except FileNotFoundError:
        return "Error: File not found."

print(count_non_empty_lines("example.txt"))
```

3. **Challenge 3: Count Lines Containing a Specific Word**

- Count the number of lines that contain a specific word or phrase.

Example:

```python
Copy code
def count_lines_with_word(file_name, word):
    try:
        with open(file_name, "r") as file:
            return sum(1 for line in file if word in line)
    except FileNotFoundError:
        return "Error: File not found."

print(count_lines_with_word("example.txt", "Python"))
```

Challenge Set 24: Reverse Content of a File

1. **Challenge 1: Reverse Entire File Content**
   - Reverse the entire content of the file and save it to a new file.

Example:

```python
Copy code
def reverse_file_content(input_file, output_file):
    try:
        with open(input_file, "r") as file:
            content = file.read()
        with open(output_file, "w") as file:
```

```
        file.write(content[::-1])
        print(f"Reversed content saved to
{output_file}")
    except FileNotFoundError:
        print("Error: File not found.")
```

```
reverse_file_content("example.txt", "reversed.txt")
```

2. **Challenge 2: Reverse Lines in a File**
   - o   Reverse the order of lines in a file and save it
     to a new file.

Example:

```python
Copy code
def reverse_lines(input_file, output_file):
    try:
        with open(input_file, "r") as file:
            lines = file.readlines()
        with open(output_file, "w") as file:
            for line in reversed(lines):
                file.write(line)
        print(f"Reversed lines saved to {output_file}")
    except FileNotFoundError:
        print("Error: File not found.")
```

```
reverse_lines("example.txt", "reversed_lines.txt")
```

3. **Challenge 3: Reverse Each Line Individually**

- o Reverse the content of each line while maintaining the order of lines.

Example:

```python
Copy code
def reverse_each_line(input_file, output_file):
    try:
        with open(input_file, "r") as file:
            lines = file.readlines()
        with open(output_file, "w") as file:
            for line in lines:
                file.write(line[::-1])
        print(f"Each line reversed and saved to {output_file}")
    except FileNotFoundError:
        print("Error: File not found.")

reverse_each_line("example.txt",
"reversed_each_line.txt")
```

Challenge Set 25: CSV Data Processor

1. **Challenge 1: Sum of a Column**
   - o Write a program to calculate the sum of values in a specific column of a CSV file.

Example:

```python
Copy code
```

```python
import csv

def sum_column(file_name, column_name):
    try:
        with open(file_name, "r") as file:
            reader = csv.DictReader(file)
            return sum(float(row[column_name]) for
row in reader)
    except FileNotFoundError:
        return "Error: File not found."
    except KeyError:
        return "Error: Column not found."

print(sum_column("data.csv", "Sales"))
```

2. **Challenge 2: Filter Rows Based on a Condition**
   o Filter rows where a specific column meets a
     condition (e.g., greater than a value) and save
     them to a new file.

Example:

```python
Copy code
def filter_rows(file_name, output_file,
column_name, threshold):
    try:
        with open(file_name, "r") as file:
            reader = csv.DictReader(file)
            rows = [row for row in reader if
float(row[column_name]) > threshold]
```

```python
        with open(output_file, "w", newline="") as file:
            writer = csv.DictWriter(file,
fieldnames=reader.fieldnames)
            writer.writeheader()
            writer.writerows(rows)
        print(f"Filtered rows saved to {output_file}")
    except FileNotFoundError:
        print("Error: File not found.")
    except KeyError:
        print("Error: Column not found.")

filter_rows("data.csv", "filtered.csv", "Sales", 5000)
```

3. **Challenge 3: Add a New Column**
   - Add a new column to a CSV file based on existing data (e.g., calculate tax from sales).

Example:

```python
Copy code
def add_tax_column(file_name, output_file,
column_name, tax_rate):
    try:
        with open(file_name, "r") as file:
            reader = csv.DictReader(file)
            rows = []
            for row in reader:
                row["Tax"] = float(row[column_name]) *
tax_rate
```

```python
        rows.append(row)

    with open(output_file, "w", newline="") as file:
        fieldnames = reader.fieldnames + ["Tax"]
        writer = csv.DictWriter(file,
fieldnames=fieldnames)
        writer.writeheader()
        writer.writerows(rows)
    print(f"New column added and saved to
{output_file}")
  except FileNotFoundError:
    print("Error: File not found.")
  except KeyError:
    print("Error: Column not found.")

add_tax_column("data.csv", "taxed.csv", "Sales",
0.1)
```

4. **Challenge 4: Group Data by a Column**
   o Group rows based on the values of a specific
     column and save the results to separate CSV
     files.

Example:

```python
Copy code
def group_by_column(file_name, column_name):
  try:
    with open(file_name, "r") as file:
      reader = csv.DictReader(file)
```

```python
        grouped_data = {}
        for row in reader:
            key = row[column_name]
            if key not in grouped_data:
                grouped_data[key] = []
            grouped_data[key].append(row)

        for key, rows in grouped_data.items():
            with open(f"{key}_group.csv", "w",
newline="") as file:
                writer = csv.DictWriter(file,
fieldnames=reader.fieldnames)
                writer.writeheader()
                writer.writerows(rows)
        print("Data grouped into separate files.")
    except FileNotFoundError:
        print("Error: File not found.")
    except KeyError:
        print("Error: Column not found.")

group_by_column("data.csv", "Region")
```

Basic Data Structures

Stacks and Queues

Stacks and **queues** are data structures that manage elements in specific orders.

Stacks

- Operate on the **LIFO** principle (Last In, First Out).
- Example operations:
    - **Push**: Add an element to the top of the stack.
    - **Pop**: Remove and return the top element.
    - **Peek**: View the top element without removing it.
- **Example Implementation Using a List**:

python
Copy code
```python
stack = []

# Push
stack.append(10)
stack.append(20)
stack.append(30)

print(stack)  # Output: [10, 20, 30]

# Pop
print(stack.pop())  # Output: 30
print(stack)        # Output: [10, 20]
```

```python
# Peek
print(stack[-1])    # Output: 20
```

Queues

- Operate on the **FIFO** principle (First In, First Out).
- Example operations:
  - **Enqueue**: Add an element to the end of the queue.
  - **Dequeue**: Remove and return the element from the front.
- **Example Implementation Using a List**:

```python
python
Copy code
queue = []

# Enqueue
queue.append(10)
queue.append(20)
queue.append(30)

print(queue)  # Output: [10, 20, 30]

# Dequeue
print(queue.pop(0))  # Output: 10
print(queue)         # Output: [20, 30]
```

- **Using collections.deque**:
  - deque is optimized for fast insertions and deletions.

```python
Copy code
from collections import deque

queue = deque()

# Enqueue
queue.append(10)
queue.append(20)
queue.append(30)

print(queue)  # Output: deque([10, 20, 30])

# Dequeue
print(queue.popleft())  # Output: 10
print(queue)            # Output: deque([20, 30])
```

Sets and Their Operations

Sets in Python are collections of unique elements. They are unordered and do not allow duplicates.

- **Creating a Set**:

```python
Copy code
my_set = {1, 2, 3, 4}
empty_set = set()  # Use set(), not {}
```

- **Common Operations**:
  - Add elements:

    ```python
    Copy code
    my_set.add(5)
    print(my_set)  # Output: {1, 2, 3, 4, 5}
    ```

  - Remove elements:

    ```python
    Copy code
    my_set.remove(3)  # Raises KeyError if the element does not exist
    my_set.discard(6)  # No error if the element does not exist
    ```

  - Check membership:

    ```python
    Copy code
    print(2 in my_set)  # Output: True
    ```

  - Get the size:

    ```python
    Copy code
    print(len(my_set))  # Output: 4
    ```

  - Clear all elements:

    ```python
    ```

```
Copy code
my_set.clear()
print(my_set)  # Output: set()
```

Set Operations

- **Union**: Combine elements from two sets.

  python
  Copy code
  ```
  set1 = {1, 2, 3}
  set2 = {3, 4, 5}
  print(set1.union(set2))  # Output: {1, 2, 3, 4, 5}
  ```

- **Intersection**: Common elements between two sets.

  python
  Copy code
  ```
  print(set1.intersection(set2))  # Output: {3}
  ```

- **Difference**: Elements in one set but not the other.

  python
  Copy code
  ```
  print(set1.difference(set2))  # Output: {1, 2}
  ```

- **Symmetric Difference**: Elements in either set but not both.

  python
  Copy code
  ```
  print(set1.symmetric_difference(set2))  # Output:
  {1, 2, 4, 5}
  ```

- **Subset and Superset**:

```python
Copy code
print(set1.issubset(set2))  # Output: False
print(set1.issuperset({1, 2}))  # Output: True
```

Challenge Set 26: Implement a Stack

1. **Challenge 1: Basic Stack Implementation**
   - Write a class to implement a stack with push, pop, and peek methods.

   Example:

```python
Copy code
class Stack:
    def __init__(self):
        self.stack = []

    def push(self, item):
        self.stack.append(item)

    def pop(self):
        if not self.is_empty():
            return self.stack.pop()
        else:
            return "Stack is empty"

    def peek(self):
        if not self.is_empty():
```

```python
            return self.stack[-1]
        else:
            return "Stack is empty"

    def is_empty(self):
        return len(self.stack) == 0

s = Stack()
s.push(10)
s.push(20)
print(s.pop())  # Output: 20
print(s.peek())  # Output: 10
```

2. **Challenge 2: Stack with Max Size**
   o Modify the stack to include a maximum size
     and prevent overflow.

Example:

python
Copy code
```python
class Stack:
    def __init__(self, max_size):
        self.stack = []
        self.max_size = max_size

    def push(self, item):
        if len(self.stack) < self.max_size:
            self.stack.append(item)
        else:
            print("Stack overflow!")
```

```python
    def pop(self):
        if not self.is_empty():
            return self.stack.pop()
        else:
            return "Stack is empty"

    def peek(self):
        if not self.is_empty():
            return self.stack[-1]
        else:
            return "Stack is empty"

    def is_empty(self):
        return len(self.stack) == 0

s = Stack(2)
s.push(10)
s.push(20)
s.push(30)  # Output: Stack overflow!
```

3. **Challenge 3: Reverse a String Using a Stack**
   - Use a stack to reverse a given string.

Example:

```python
python
Copy code
def reverse_string(string):
    stack = []
    for char in string:
```

```python
        stack.append(char)
    reversed_str = ""
    while stack:
        reversed_str += stack.pop()
    return reversed_str

print(reverse_string("hello"))  # Output: olleh
```

4. **Challenge 4: Balanced Parentheses**
   o Use a stack to check if a string has balanced parentheses.

Example:

```python
Copy code
def is_balanced(string):
    stack = []
    for char in string:
        if char == "(":
            stack.append(char)
        elif char == ")":
            if not stack:
                return False
            stack.pop()
    return len(stack) == 0

print(is_balanced("(())"))  # Output: True
print(is_balanced("(()"))  # Output: False
```

Challenge Set 27: Unique Elements in a List

1. **Challenge 1: Remove Duplicates**
   - ○ Write a program to remove duplicate elements from a list.

   Example:

   python
   Copy code
   ```
   def remove_duplicates(lst):
       return list(set(lst))

   numbers = [1, 2, 2, 3, 4, 4, 5]
   print(remove_duplicates(numbers))  # Output: [1, 2, 3, 4, 5]
   ```

2. **Challenge 2: Retain Order While Removing Duplicates**
   - ○ Remove duplicates but retain the order of elements.

   Example:

   python
   Copy code
   ```
   def remove_duplicates_ordered(lst):
       seen = set()
       unique = []
       for item in lst:
           if item not in seen:
               seen.add(item)
               unique.append(item)
   ```

```
    return unique
```

```
numbers = [1, 2, 2, 3, 4, 4, 5]
print(remove_duplicates_ordered(numbers))  #
Output: [1, 2, 3, 4, 5]
```

3. **Challenge 3: Count Unique Elements**
   - o Write a program to count the number of unique elements in a list.

   Example:

   python
   Copy code
   ```python
   def count_unique(lst):
       return len(set(lst))
   ```

   ```
   numbers = [1, 2, 2, 3, 4, 4, 5]
   print(count_unique(numbers))  # Output: 5
   ```

4. **Challenge 4: Find Unique Elements**
   - o Write a program to find the elements that appear only once in the list.

   Example:

   python
   Copy code
   ```python
   def find_unique(lst):
       counts = {}
       for item in lst:
           counts[item] = counts.get(item, 0) + 1
   ```

```python
    return [key for key, value in counts.items() if
value == 1]

numbers = [1, 2, 2, 3, 4, 4, 5]
print(find_unique(numbers))  # Output: [1, 3, 5]
```

Challenge Set 28: Simple Queue System

1. **Challenge 1: Implement a Queue**
   o Create a class to implement a basic queue
     with enqueue, dequeue, and peek operations.

Example:

python
Copy code
```python
class Queue:
    def __init__(self):
        self.queue = []

    def enqueue(self, item):
        self.queue.append(item)

    def dequeue(self):
        if not self.is_empty():
            return self.queue.pop(0)
        else:
            return "Queue is empty"

    def peek(self):
        if not self.is_empty():
            return self.queue[0]
```

```python
        else:
            return "Queue is empty"

    def is_empty(self):
        return len(self.queue) == 0

q = Queue()
q.enqueue(10)
q.enqueue(20)
print(q.dequeue())  # Output: 10
print(q.peek())     # Output: 20
```

2. **Challenge 2: Bounded Queue**
   - Modify the queue to include a maximum size and prevent overflow.

Example:

```python
python
Copy code
class BoundedQueue:
    def __init__(self, max_size):
        self.queue = []
        self.max_size = max_size

    def enqueue(self, item):
        if len(self.queue) < self.max_size:
            self.queue.append(item)
        else:
            print("Queue overflow!")
```

```python
    def dequeue(self):
        if not self.is_empty():
            return self.queue.pop(0)
        else:
            return "Queue is empty"

    def is_empty(self):
        return len(self.queue) == 0

q = BoundedQueue(2)
q.enqueue(10)
q.enqueue(20)
q.enqueue(30)  # Output: Queue overflow!
```

3. **Challenge 3: Circular Queue**
   o Implement a circular queue using a list.

Example:

```python
python
Copy code
class CircularQueue:
    def __init__(self, max_size):
        self.queue = [None] * max_size
        self.max_size = max_size
        self.front = self.rear = -1

    def enqueue(self, item):
        if (self.rear + 1) % self.max_size == self.front:
            print("Queue overflow!")
        elif self.front == -1:  # Empty queue
```

```python
            self.front = self.rear = 0
            self.queue[self.rear] = item
        else:
            self.rear = (self.rear + 1) % self.max_size
            self.queue[self.rear] = item

    def dequeue(self):
        if self.front == -1:
            return "Queue is empty"
        elif self.front == self.rear:  # Only one element
left
            item = self.queue[self.front]
            self.front = self.rear = -1
            return item
        else:
            item = self.queue[self.front]
            self.front = (self.front + 1) % self.max_size
            return item

    def display(self):
        if self.front == -1:
            print("Queue is empty")
        else:
            i = self.front
            while True:
                print(self.queue[i], end=" ")
                if i == self.rear:
                    break
                i = (i + 1) % self.max_size
            print()
```

```python
cq = CircularQueue(3)
cq.enqueue(10)
cq.enqueue(20)
cq.enqueue(30)
cq.display()  # Output: 10 20 30
print(cq.dequeue())  # Output: 10
cq.enqueue(40)
cq.display()  # Output: 20 30 40
```

4. **Challenge 4: Priority Queue**
   - Implement a priority queue where elements with higher priority are dequeued first.

Example:

python
Copy code
```python
import heapq

class PriorityQueue:
    def __init__(self):
        self.queue = []

    def enqueue(self, item, priority):
        heapq.heappush(self.queue, (priority, item))

    def dequeue(self):
        if self.queue:
            return heapq.heappop(self.queue)[1]
        else:
            return "Queue is empty"
```

```
pq = PriorityQueue()
pq.enqueue("Task 1", 2)
pq.enqueue("Task 2", 1)
pq.enqueue("Task 3", 3)
print(pq.dequeue())  # Output: Task 2 (highest
priority)
```

Introduction to Object-Oriented Programming
Classes and Objects

Classes are blueprints for creating objects, and **objects** are instances of those classes. They help organize data and behavior in a structured way.

1. Defining a Class

```python
python
Copy code
class MyClass:
    # Class attributes (shared across all instances)
    class_attribute = "I am a class attribute"

    def __init__(self, value):
        # Instance attributes (specific to each instance)
        self.instance_attribute = value

# Creating an object (instance)
obj = MyClass("I am an instance attribute")
print(obj.class_attribute)      # Output: I am a class attribute
print(obj.instance_attribute)   # Output: I am an instance attribute
```

Methods and Attributes

1. Instance Methods

- Defined using def and require self as the first parameter.
- Operate on an object's data (instance attributes).

Example:

```python
Copy code
class Person:
    def __init__(self, name, age):
        self.name = name
        self.age = age

    def greet(self):
        print(f"Hello, my name is {self.name} and I am {self.age} years old.")

p = Person("Alice", 30)
p.greet()  # Output: Hello, my name is Alice and I am 30 years old.
```

2. Class Methods

- Defined using @classmethod decorator.
- Operate on class-level data and take cls as the first parameter.

Example:

```python
Copy code
class Person:
    population = 0

    def __init__(self, name):
        self.name = name
```

```
        Person.population += 1

    @classmethod
    def get_population(cls):
        return cls.population

p1 = Person("Alice")
p2 = Person("Bob")
print(Person.get_population())  # Output: 2
```
3. Static Methods

- Defined using @staticmethod decorator.
- Do not operate on instance or class data (no self or cls).

Example:

```
python
Copy code
class Calculator:
    @staticmethod
    def add(a, b):
        return a + b

print(Calculator.add(5, 3))  # Output: 8
```
4. Special (Dunder) Methods

- Special methods provide custom behavior for built-in operations.

Example:

```python
Copy code
class Point:
    def __init__(self, x, y):
        self.x = x
        self.y = y

    def __add__(self, other):
        return Point(self.x + other.x, self.y + other.y)

    def __str__(self):
        return f"({self.x}, {self.y})"

p1 = Point(1, 2)
p2 = Point(3, 4)
p3 = p1 + p2
print(p3)  # Output: (4, 6)
```

Challenge Set 29: Create a Simple Class

1. **Challenge 1: Define a Car Class**
   - Write a Car class with attributes make, model, and year. Add a method to display the car's details.

   Example:

   ```python
   Copy code
   class Car:
       def __init__(self, make, model, year):
   ```

```python
        self.make = make
        self.model = model
        self.year = year

    def display_info(self):
        print(f"{self.year} {self.make} {self.model}")

car = Car("Toyota", "Corolla", 2020)
car.display_info()  # Output: 2020 Toyota Corolla
```

2. **Challenge 2: Add a Method to Start the Car**
   - Extend the Car class with a start() method that prints a message.

Example:

```python
python
Copy code
class Car:
    def __init__(self, make, model, year):
        self.make = make
        self.model = model
        self.year = year

    def start(self):
        print(f"The {self.year} {self.make} {self.model} is starting...")

car = Car("Honda", "Civic", 2019)
car.start()  # Output: The 2019 Honda Civic is starting...
```

3. **Challenge 3: Add a Class Attribute**
   - o Add a class attribute total_cars to track the number of Car instances created.

Example:

```python
Copy code
class Car:
    total_cars = 0

    def __init__(self, make, model, year):
        self.make = make
        self.model = model
        self.year = year
        Car.total_cars += 1

car1 = Car("Toyota", "Corolla", 2020)
car2 = Car("Honda", "Civic", 2019)
print(Car.total_cars)  # Output: 2
```

Challenge Set 30: Bank Account Simulator

1. **Challenge 1: Define a BankAccount Class**
   - o Create a BankAccount class with attributes account_number and balance. Add methods to deposit and withdraw money.

Example:

```python
Copy code
```

```python
class BankAccount:
    def __init__(self, account_number, balance=0):
        self.account_number = account_number
        self.balance = balance

    def deposit(self, amount):
        self.balance += amount
        print(f"Deposited ${amount}. New balance: ${self.balance}")

    def withdraw(self, amount):
        if amount > self.balance:
            print("Insufficient funds.")
        else:
            self.balance -= amount
            print(f"Withdrew ${amount}. New balance: ${self.balance}")

account = BankAccount("123456")
account.deposit(500)
account.withdraw(200)
```

2. **Challenge 2: Add Interest**
   - Add a method to apply interest to the balance.

Example:

python
Copy code
```python
class BankAccount:
```

```python
    def __init__(self, account_number, balance=0,
interest_rate=0.01):
        self.account_number = account_number
        self.balance = balance
        self.interest_rate = interest_rate

    def apply_interest(self):
        self.balance += self.balance * self.interest_rate
        print(f"Interest applied. New balance:
${self.balance:.2f}")

account = BankAccount("123456", 1000, 0.02)
account.apply_interest()  # Output: Interest applied.
New balance: $1020.00
```

3. **Challenge 3: Transaction History**
   o Add a transaction_history attribute to track all deposits and withdrawals.

Example:

```python
python
Copy code
class BankAccount:
    def __init__(self, account_number, balance=0):
        self.account_number = account_number
        self.balance = balance
        self.transaction_history = []

    def deposit(self, amount):
        self.balance += amount
```

```python
        self.transaction_history.append(f"Deposited
${amount}")
        print(f"Deposited ${amount}. New balance:
${self.balance}")

    def withdraw(self, amount):
        if amount > self.balance:
            print("Insufficient funds.")
        else:
            self.balance -= amount
            self.transaction_history.append(f"Withdrew
${amount}")
            print(f"Withdrew ${amount}. New balance:
${self.balance}")

    def show_transaction_history(self):
        print("Transaction History:")
        for transaction in self.transaction_history:
            print(transaction)

account = BankAccount("123456")
account.deposit(100)
account.withdraw(50)
account.show_transaction_history()
```

Working with Libraries

Using the Math Library

The Python math library provides various mathematical functions and constants.

1. Importing the Library

python
Copy code
```
import math
```
2. Common Functions

- **Constants**:

  python
  Copy code
  ```
  print(math.pi)   # Output: 3.141592653589793
  print(math.e)    # Output: 2.718281828459045
  ```

- **Basic Operations**:

  python
  Copy code
  ```
  print(math.sqrt(16))    # Output: 4.0
  print(math.pow(2, 3))   # Output: 8.0
  print(math.log(100, 10)) # Output: 2.0
  print(math.factorial(5)) # Output: 120
  ```

- **Trigonometric Functions**:

  python

```
Copy code
print(math.sin(math.pi / 2))  # Output: 1.0
print(math.cos(0))            # Output: 1.0
print(math.degrees(math.pi))  # Output: 180.0
print(math.radians(180))      # Output:
3.141592653589793
```

- **Rounding Functions**:

python
```
Copy code
print(math.ceil(4.3))  # Output: 5
print(math.floor(4.7)) # Output: 4
print(math.trunc(4.9)) # Output: 4
```

Generating Random Numbers

The random module allows you to generate random numbers and perform random operations.

1. Importing the Module

python
```
Copy code
import random
```

2. Common Functions

- **Generate Random Numbers**:

python
Copy code

```python
print(random.random())  # Output: Random float
between 0.0 and 1.0
print(random.randint(1, 10))  # Output: Random
integer between 1 and 10
print(random.uniform(1.5, 7.5))  # Output: Random
float between 1.5 and 7.5
```

- **Choose Random Items**:

python
Copy code
```python
items = [1, 2, 3, 4, 5]
print(random.choice(items))  # Output: Random
item from the list
print(random.choices(items, k=3))  # Output: List of
3 random items
```

- **Shuffle a List**:

python
Copy code
```python
random.shuffle(items)
print(items)  # Output: List shuffled randomly
```

Challenge Set 31: Random Password Generator

1. **Challenge 1: Generate a Simple Password**
   - Create a program that generates a password
     of a specified length using letters.

   Example:

```python
Copy code
import random
import string

def generate_password(length):
    letters = string.ascii_letters
    return ''.join(random.choices(letters, k=length))

print(generate_password(8))  # Output: Random 8-character password
```

2. **Challenge 2: Password with Letters and Numbers**
   ○ Modify the program to include letters and digits.

   Example:

```python
Copy code
def generate_password(length):
    characters = string.ascii_letters + string.digits
    return ''.join(random.choices(characters, k=length))

print(generate_password(10))  # Output: Random 10-character password
```

3. **Challenge 3: Strong Password**

o Include letters, digits, and special characters, ensuring at least one of each.

Example:

```python
Copy code
def generate_strong_password(length):
    if length < 4:
        return "Password must be at least 4 characters long"

    all_characters = string.ascii_letters + string.digits + string.punctuation
    password = [
        random.choice(string.ascii_lowercase),
        random.choice(string.ascii_uppercase),
        random.choice(string.digits),
        random.choice(string.punctuation),
    ]
    password += random.choices(all_characters, k=length - 4)
    random.shuffle(password)
    return ''.join(password)

print(generate_strong_password(12))  # Output: Random strong 12-character password
```

Challenge Set 32: Area of a Circle

1. ## Challenge 1: Calculate the Area
   o Write a program to calculate the area of a circle given its radius.

   Formula:

   $Area=\pi r2\text{Area} = \pi r^2 Area=\pi r2$

   Example:

   python
   Copy code
   ```
   import math

   def circle_area(radius):
       return math.pi * math.pow(radius, 2)

   print(circle_area(5))  # Output: 78.53981633974483
   ```

2. ## Challenge 2: User Input
   o Modify the program to take the radius as input from the user.

   Example:

   python
   Copy code
   ```
   def circle_area():
       radius = float(input("Enter the radius of the circle: "))
   ```

```python
    area = math.pi * math.pow(radius, 2)
    print(f"The area of the circle is: {area:.2f}")

circle_area()
```

3. **Challenge 3: Validate Input**
   o Ensure the radius is a positive number.

Example:

```python
python
Copy code
def circle_area():
    while True:
        try:
            radius = float(input("Enter the radius of the circle: "))
            if radius <= 0:
                print("Radius must be a positive number. Try again.")
                continue
            area = math.pi * math.pow(radius, 2)
            print(f"The area of the circle is: {area:.2f}")
            break
        except ValueError:
            print("Invalid input. Please enter a valid number.")

circle_area()
```

Basic Algorithms

Sorting Algorithms

Sorting algorithms arrange elements of a list or array in a specific order (ascending or descending).

1. Bubble Sort

- Compares adjacent elements and swaps them if they are in the wrong order.
- Repeats until the list is sorted.
- **Time Complexity**: $O(n2)O(n^2)O(n2)$ in the worst case.

Example:

```python
Copy code
def bubble_sort(arr):
    n = len(arr)
    for i in range(n - 1):
        for j in range(n - i - 1):
            if arr[j] > arr[j + 1]:
                arr[j], arr[j + 1] = arr[j + 1], arr[j]
    return arr

numbers = [64, 34, 25, 12, 22, 11, 90]
print(bubble_sort(numbers))  # Output: [11, 12, 22, 25, 34, 64, 90]
```

2. Merge Sort

- Divides the list into two halves, sorts each half, and then merges them.
- **Time Complexity**: $O(n\log n)$O(n \log n)O(nlogn).

Example:

```python
Copy code
def merge_sort(arr):
    if len(arr) > 1:
        mid = len(arr) // 2
        left = arr[:mid]
        right = arr[mid:]

        merge_sort(left)
        merge_sort(right)

        i = j = k = 0
        while i < len(left) and j < len(right):
            if left[i] < right[j]:
                arr[k] = left[i]
                i += 1
            else:
                arr[k] = right[j]
                j += 1
            k += 1

        while i < len(left):
            arr[k] = left[i]
            i += 1
            k += 1
```

```
    while j < len(right):
        arr[k] = right[j]
        j += 1
        k += 1
    return arr

numbers = [38, 27, 43, 3, 9, 82, 10]
print(merge_sort(numbers))  # Output: [3, 9, 10, 27, 38,
43, 82]
```

Searching Algorithms

Searching algorithms locate an element within a list.

1. Linear Search

- Checks each element one by one until the target is found or the list ends.
- **Time Complexity**: $O(n)O(n)O(n)$.

Example:

```python
Copy code
def linear_search(arr, target):
    for i, value in enumerate(arr):
        if value == target:
            return i
    return -1


numbers = [10, 20, 30, 40, 50]
print(linear_search(numbers, 30))  # Output: 2
```

2. Binary Search

- Works on sorted lists by repeatedly dividing the search interval in half.
- **Time Complexity**: $O(\log n)$.

Example:

```python
Copy code
def binary_search(arr, target):
    low, high = 0, len(arr) - 1
    while low <= high:
        mid = (low + high) // 2
        if arr[mid] == target:
            return mid
        elif arr[mid] < target:
            low = mid + 1
        else:
            high = mid - 1
    return -1
```

numbers = [10, 20, 30, 40, 50]
print(binary_search(numbers, 30)) # Output: 2

Challenge Set 33: Bubble Sort Implementation

1. **Challenge 1: Basic Bubble Sort**
   - Implement a bubble sort to sort a list in ascending order.

   Example:

   ```python
   Copy code
   def bubble_sort(arr):
       n = len(arr)
       for i in range(n - 1):
           for j in range(n - i - 1):
               if arr[j] > arr[j + 1]:
                   arr[j], arr[j + 1] = arr[j + 1], arr[j]
       return arr

   numbers = [5, 3, 8, 6, 2]
   print(bubble_sort(numbers))  # Output: [2, 3, 5, 6, 8]
   ```

2. **Challenge 2: Bubble Sort in Descending Order**
   - Modify the algorithm to sort the list in descending order.

   Example:

```python
Copy code
def bubble_sort_descending(arr):
    n = len(arr)
    for i in range(n - 1):
        for j in range(n - i - 1):
            if arr[j] < arr[j + 1]:
                arr[j], arr[j + 1] = arr[j + 1], arr[j]
    return arr

numbers = [5, 3, 8, 6, 2]
print(bubble_sort_descending(numbers))  # Output: [8, 6, 5, 3, 2]
```

3. **Challenge 3: Optimized Bubble Sort**
   o Stop the algorithm early if no swaps are made in an iteration.

Example:

```python
Copy code
def optimized_bubble_sort(arr):
    n = len(arr)
    for i in range(n - 1):
        swapped = False
        for j in range(n - i - 1):
            if arr[j] > arr[j + 1]:
                arr[j], arr[j + 1] = arr[j + 1], arr[j]
                swapped = True
        if not swapped:
```

```
        break
    return arr

numbers = [5, 3, 8, 6, 2]
print(optimized_bubble_sort(numbers))  # Output:
[2, 3, 5, 6, 8]
```

Challenge Set 34: Binary Search Algorithm

1. **Challenge 1: Basic Binary Search**
   o Implement a binary search function for a
     sorted list.

   Example:

```python
Copy code
def binary_search(arr, target):
    low, high = 0, len(arr) - 1
    while low <= high:
        mid = (low + high) // 2
        if arr[mid] == target:
            return mid
        elif arr[mid] < target:
            low = mid + 1
        else:
            high = mid - 1
    return -1

numbers = [2, 4, 6, 8, 10]
print(binary_search(numbers, 6))  # Output: 2
```

2. **Challenge 2: Binary Search with Recursion**
   o Implement a recursive version of binary search.

Example:

```python
Copy code
def binary_search_recursive(arr, target, low, high):
    if low > high:
        return -1
    mid = (low + high) // 2
    if arr[mid] == target:
        return mid
    elif arr[mid] < target:
        return binary_search_recursive(arr, target, mid + 1, high)
    else:
        return binary_search_recursive(arr, target, low, mid - 1)

numbers = [2, 4, 6, 8, 10]
print(binary_search_recursive(numbers, 6, 0, len(numbers) - 1))  # Output: 2
```

3. **Challenge 3: Find Closest Element**
   o Modify the binary search to find the closest value to the target.

Example:

```python
Copy code
def find_closest(arr, target):
    low, high = 0, len(arr) - 1
    closest = arr[0]
    while low <= high:
        mid = (low + high) // 2
        if abs(arr[mid] - target) < abs(closest - target):
            closest = arr[mid]
        if arr[mid] < target:
            low = mid + 1
        else:
            high = mid - 1
    return closest

numbers = [1, 3, 5, 8, 12]
print(find_closest(numbers, 7))  # Output: 8
```

Intermediate Challenges

Nested Loops

Nested loops are loops inside other loops, useful for working with multi-dimensional data or creating patterns.

Example 1: Multiplication Table

```python
Copy code
for i in range(1, 6):
    for j in range(1, 6):
        print(f"{i * j:2}", end=" ")
    print()
```

Output:

```
Copy code
 1  2  3  4  5
 2  4  6  8 10
 3  6  9 12 15
 4  8 12 16 20
 5 10 15 20 25
```

Example 2: Printing a Grid

```python
Copy code
rows = 3
cols = 4
for i in range(rows):
    for j in range(cols):
        print(f"({i}, {j})", end=" ")
```

print()

Output:

scss
Copy code
(0, 0) (0, 1) (0, 2) (0, 3)
(1, 0) (1, 1) (1, 2) (1, 3)
(2, 0) (2, 1) (2, 2) (2, 3)
Pattern Printing

Pattern printing involves using nested loops to display specific arrangements of symbols.

Example 1: Right-Angled Triangle

```python
Copy code
rows = 5
for i in range(1, rows + 1):
    print("*" * i)
```

Output:

```markdown
Copy code
*
**
***
****
*****
```

Example 2: Pyramid

```python
Copy code
rows = 5
for i in range(1, rows + 1):
    print(" " * (rows - i) + "*" * (2 * i - 1))
```

Output:

```markdown
Copy code
    *
   ***
  *****
 *******
*********
```

Challenge Set 35: Diamond Pattern

1. **Challenge 1: Print a Diamond Pattern**
   - Create a program that prints a diamond pattern using *.

   Example:

   ```python
   Copy code
   rows = 5
   for i in range(1, rows + 1):
       print(" " * (rows - i) + "*" * (2 * i - 1))
   for i in range(rows - 1, 0, -1):
       print(" " * (rows - i) + "*" * (2 * i - 1))
   ```

Output:

```markdown
Copy code
    *
   ***
  *****
 *******
*********
 *******
  *****
   ***
    *
```

2. **Challenge 2: Hollow Diamond**
   - Modify the diamond pattern to make it hollow.

Example:

```python
Copy code
rows = 5
for i in range(1, rows + 1):
    if i == 1:
        print(" " * (rows - i) + "*")
    else:
        print(" " * (rows - i) + "*" + " " * (2 * i - 3) +
"*")
for i in range(rows - 1, 0, -1):
    if i == 1:
```

```
    print(" " * (rows - i) + "*")
  else:
    print(" " * (rows - i) + "*" + " " * (2 * i - 3) +
"*")
```

Output:

```markdown
Copy code
    *
   * *
  *   *
 *     *
*       *
*       *
*       *
 *     *
  *   *
   * *
    *
```

Challenge Set 36: Spiral Matrix

1. **Challenge 1: Generate a Spiral Matrix**
   o Write a program to generate a square spiral matrix.

Example:

```python
Copy code
def generate_spiral(n):
    matrix = [[0] * n for _ in range(n)]
    top, left = 0, 0
```

```python
    bottom, right = n - 1, n - 1
    num = 1

    while top <= bottom and left <= right:
        for i in range(left, right + 1):
            matrix[top][i] = num
            num += 1
        top += 1

        for i in range(top, bottom + 1):
            matrix[i][right] = num
            num += 1
        right -= 1

        for i in range(right, left - 1, -1):
            matrix[bottom][i] = num
            num += 1
        bottom -= 1

        for i in range(bottom, top - 1, -1):
            matrix[i][left] = num
            num += 1
        left += 1

    return matrix

n = 5
spiral = generate_spiral(n)
for row in spiral:
    print(row)
```

Output:

csharp
Copy code
[1, 2, 3, 4, 5]
[16, 17, 18, 19, 6]
[15, 24, 25, 20, 7]
[14, 23, 22, 21, 8]
[13, 12, 11, 10, 9]

2. **Challenge 2: Spiral Print of an Existing Matrix**
   o Write a program to print an existing matrix in a spiral order.

Example:

python
Copy code

```python
def spiral_print(matrix):
    rows, cols = len(matrix), len(matrix[0])
    top, left = 0, 0
    bottom, right = rows - 1, cols - 1

    while top <= bottom and left <= right:
        for i in range(left, right + 1):
            print(matrix[top][i], end=" ")
        top += 1

        for i in range(top, bottom + 1):
            print(matrix[i][right], end=" ")
        right -= 1
```

```python
        if top <= bottom:
            for i in range(right, left - 1, -1):
                print(matrix[bottom][i], end=" ")
            bottom -= 1

        if left <= right:
            for i in range(bottom, top - 1, -1):
                print(matrix[i][left], end=" ")
            left += 1

matrix = [
    [1, 2, 3, 4],
    [5, 6, 7, 8],
    [9, 10, 11, 12],
    [13, 14, 15, 16]
]
spiral_print(matrix)
```

Output:

```
Copy code
1 2 3 4 8 12 16 15 14 13 9 5 6 7 11 10
```

Games and Fun Challenges
Building Simple Games

Simple games are a great way to practice programming concepts, such as conditionals, loops, and input/output handling.

Challenge Set 37: Guess the Number

1. **Challenge 1: Single Player**
   - Create a game where the computer picks a random number, and the player has to guess it.

   Example:

   python
   Copy code
   ```python
   import random

   def guess_the_number():
       number = random.randint(1, 100)
       print("I have picked a number between 1 and 100. Try to guess it!")

       while True:
           guess = int(input("Enter your guess: "))
           if guess < number:
               print("Too low! Try again.")
           elif guess > number:
               print("Too high! Try again.")
   ```

```python
        else:
            print("Congratulations! You guessed the number!")
            break

guess_the_number()
```

2. **Challenge 2: Add a Guess Counter**
   - Track the number of attempts it takes to guess the number.

Example:

```python
python
Copy code
def guess_the_number():
    number = random.randint(1, 100)
    attempts = 0
    print("I have picked a number between 1 and 100. Try to guess it!")

    while True:
        guess = int(input("Enter your guess: "))
        attempts += 1
        if guess < number:
            print("Too low! Try again.")
        elif guess > number:
            print("Too high! Try again.")
        else:
            print(f"Congratulations! You guessed the number in {attempts} attempts!")
```

```
        break

guess_the_number()
```

3. **Challenge 3: Multiplayer Mode**
   - Add a mode where two players compete to guess the number, taking turns.

Challenge Set 38: Rock, Paper, Scissors

1. **Challenge 1: Play Against the Computer**
   - Implement a basic rock-paper-scissors game where the player competes against the computer.

   Example:

   ```python
   Copy code
   import random

   def rock_paper_scissors():
       options = ["rock", "paper", "scissors"]
       computer_choice = random.choice(options)

       player_choice = input("Enter rock, paper, or scissors: ").lower()
       if player_choice not in options:
           print("Invalid choice. Try again.")
           return
   ```

```python
        print(f"Computer chose: {computer_choice}")

    if player_choice == computer_choice:
        print("It's a tie!")
    elif (player_choice == "rock" and
computer_choice == "scissors") or \
        (player_choice == "scissors" and
computer_choice == "paper") or \
        (player_choice == "paper" and
computer_choice == "rock"):
        print("You win!")
    else:
        print("You lose!")

rock_paper_scissors()
```

2. **Challenge 2: Best of Three**
   - Modify the game to allow a "best of three" competition.

   Example:

   python
   Copy code
```python
def best_of_three():
    options = ["rock", "paper", "scissors"]
    player_score, computer_score = 0, 0

    for _ in range(3):
        computer_choice = random.choice(options)
```

```python
        player_choice = input("Enter rock, paper, or
scissors: ").lower()
        if player_choice not in options:
            print("Invalid choice. Try again.")
            continue

        print(f"Computer chose: {computer_choice}")
        if player_choice == computer_choice:
            print("It's a tie!")
        elif (player_choice == "rock" and
computer_choice == "scissors") or \
            (player_choice == "scissors" and
computer_choice == "paper") or \
            (player_choice == "paper" and
computer_choice == "rock"):
            print("You win this round!")
            player_score += 1
        else:
            print("Computer wins this round!")
            computer_score += 1

    if player_score > computer_score:
        print("You win the best of three!")
    elif player_score < computer_score:
        print("Computer wins the best of three!")
    else:
        print("It's a tie!")

best_of_three()
```

Challenge Set 39: Tic Tac Toe

1. **Challenge 1: Two-Player Mode**
   - Create a basic Tic Tac Toe game for two players.

   Example:

```python
Copy code
def print_board(board):
    for row in board:
        print(" | ".join(row))
        print("-" * 5)

def check_winner(board, marker):
    for row in board:
        if all(cell == marker for cell in row):
            return True
    for col in range(3):
        if all(row[col] == marker for row in board):
            return True
    if all(board[i][i] == marker for i in range(3)) or \
        all(board[i][2 - i] == marker for i in range(3)):
        return True
    return False

def tic_tac_toe():
    board = [[" " for _ in range(3)] for _ in range(3)]
    players = ["X", "O"]
    turn = 0

    for _ in range(9):
```

```python
        print_board(board)
        marker = players[turn % 2]
        print(f"Player {marker}'s turn.")
        row = int(input("Enter row (0-2): "))
        col = int(input("Enter column (0-2): "))

        if board[row][col] == " ":
            board[row][col] = marker
            if check_winner(board, marker):
                print_board(board)
                print(f"Player {marker} wins!")
                return
            turn += 1
        else:
            print("Cell is already occupied. Try again.")

    print_board(board)
    print("It's a tie!")

tic_tac_toe()
```

2. **Challenge 2: AI Opponent**
   o   Implement a simple AI for the computer to play against the user.

Example:

python
Copy code

```python
import random

def ai_move(board):
    empty_cells = [(r, c) for r in range(3) for c in
range(3) if board[r][c] == " "]
    return random.choice(empty_cells)

def tic_tac_toe_with_ai():
    board = [[" " for _ in range(3)] for _ in range(3)]
    players = ["X", "O"]
    turn = 0

    for _ in range(9):
        print_board(board)
        if turn % 2 == 0:
            print("Your turn (X).")
            row = int(input("Enter row (0-2): "))
            col = int(input("Enter column (0-2): "))
        else:
            print("Computer's turn (O).")
            row, col = ai_move(board)

        if board[row][col] == " ":
            board[row][col] = players[turn % 2]
            if check_winner(board, players[turn % 2]):
                print_board(board)
                print(f"Player {players[turn % 2]} wins!")
                return
            turn += 1
        else:
            print("Cell is already occupied. Try again.")
```

```python
        print_board(board)
        print("It's a tie!")

tic_tac_toe_with_ai()
```

Mini Projects

Combining Concepts in Small Projects

These projects combine various programming concepts like input/output, loops, conditionals, and data structures to create functional applications.

Challenge Set 40: To-Do List Application

1. **Challenge 1: Basic To-Do List**
   - Create an app where users can add tasks, view the list, and mark tasks as complete.

   Example:

   ```python
   Copy code
   def to_do_list():
       tasks = []

       while True:
           print("\nTo-Do List Menu:")
           print("1. Add Task")
           print("2. View Tasks")
           print("3. Mark Task as Complete")
           print("4. Exit")
           choice = input("Choose an option: ")

           if choice == "1":
               task = input("Enter the task: ")
   ```

```python
            tasks.append({"task": task, "completed": False})
            print("Task added.")
        elif choice == "2":
            print("\nTasks:")
            for i, task in enumerate(tasks):
                status = "Done" if task["completed"] else "Pending"
                print(f"{i + 1}. {task['task']} - {status}")
        elif choice == "3":
            task_num = int(input("Enter the task number to mark as complete: ")) - 1
            if 0 <= task_num < len(tasks):
                tasks[task_num]["completed"] = True
                print("Task marked as complete.")
            else:
                print("Invalid task number.")
        elif choice == "4":
            print("Exiting To-Do List.")
            break
        else:
            print("Invalid choice. Try again.")

to_do_list()
```

Challenge Set 41: Basic Calculator App

1. **Challenge 1: Basic Operations**
   - Create a calculator that performs addition, subtraction, multiplication, and division.

Example:

```python
Copy code
def calculator():
    while True:
        print("\nCalculator Menu:")
        print("1. Add")
        print("2. Subtract")
        print("3. Multiply")
        print("4. Divide")
        print("5. Exit")
        choice = input("Choose an option: ")

        if choice in ["1", "2", "3", "4"]:
            num1 = float(input("Enter the first number: "))
            num2 = float(input("Enter the second number: "))

            if choice == "1":
                print(f"Result: {num1 + num2}")
            elif choice == "2":
                print(f"Result: {num1 - num2}")
            elif choice == "3":
                print(f"Result: {num1 * num2}")
            elif choice == "4":
                if num2 != 0:
                    print(f"Result: {num1 / num2}")
                else:
```

```
            print("Error: Division by zero is not
allowed.")
        elif choice == "5":
            print("Exiting Calculator.")
            break
        else:
            print("Invalid choice. Try again.")

calculator()
```

2. **Challenge 2: Add Advanced Features**
   o Add advanced operations like exponentiation, modulus, and square root.

Example:

```python
Copy code
import math

def advanced_calculator():
    while True:
        print("\nAdvanced Calculator Menu:")
        print("1. Add")
        print("2. Subtract")
        print("3. Multiply")
        print("4. Divide")
        print("5. Exponentiation")
        print("6. Modulus")
        print("7. Square Root")
        print("8. Exit")
```

```python
choice = input("Choose an option: ")

if choice in ["1", "2", "3", "4", "5", "6"]:
    num1 = float(input("Enter the first number: "))
    num2 = float(input("Enter the second number: "))

    if choice == "1":
        print(f"Result: {num1 + num2}")
    elif choice == "2":
        print(f"Result: {num1 - num2}")
    elif choice == "3":
        print(f"Result: {num1 * num2}")
    elif choice == "4":
        if num2 != 0:
            print(f"Result: {num1 / num2}")
        else:
            print("Error: Division by zero is not allowed.")
    elif choice == "5":
        print(f"Result: {num1 ** num2}")
    elif choice == "6":
        print(f"Result: {num1 % num2}")
elif choice == "7":
    num = float(input("Enter the number: "))
    if num >= 0:
        print(f"Result: {math.sqrt(num)}")
    else:
        print("Error: Square root of negative numbers is not allowed.")
```

```python
    elif choice == "8":
        print("Exiting Advanced Calculator.")
        break
    else:
        print("Invalid choice. Try again.")

advanced_calculator()
```

Challenge Set 42: Simple Quiz Game

1. **Challenge 1: Create a Basic Quiz**
   - Create a multiple-choice quiz where users answer questions and receive a score at the end.

   Example:

```python
python
Copy code
def quiz_game():
    questions = [
        {"question": "What is the capital of France?", "options": ["Paris", "London", "Berlin", "Rome"], "answer": "Paris"},
        {"question": "What is 5 + 3?", "options": ["5", "8", "10", "15"], "answer": "8"},
        {"question": "What is the largest planet in our solar system?", "options": ["Earth", "Mars", "Jupiter", "Venus"], "answer": "Jupiter"},
    ]
```

```python
    score = 0
    for i, q in enumerate(questions):
        print(f"\nQuestion {i + 1}: {q['question']}")
        for j, option in enumerate(q["options"]):
            print(f"{j + 1}. {option}")
        answer = input("Your answer (1-4): ")
        if q["options"][int(answer) - 1] == q["answer"]:
            print("Correct!")
            score += 1
        else:
            print(f"Wrong! The correct answer was
{q['answer']}.")

    print(f"\nYou scored {score}/{len(questions)}.")

quiz_game()
```

2. **Challenge 2: Add Difficulty Levels**
   - Add a menu for selecting difficulty levels, with easier levels showing fewer options and harder levels showing more.
3. **Challenge 3: Track High Scores**
   - Keep track of the user's highest scores and display them at the end.

Example:

```python
python
Copy code
def quiz_game_with_scores():
    questions = [
```

```python
    {"question": "What is the capital of France?",
"options": ["Paris", "London", "Berlin", "Rome"],
"answer": "Paris"},
    {"question": "What is 5 + 3?", "options": ["5",
"8", "10", "15"], "answer": "8"},
    {"question": "What is the largest planet in our
solar system?", "options": ["Earth", "Mars",
"Jupiter", "Venus"], "answer": "Jupiter"},
    ]

high_score = 0

while True:
    score = 0
    for i, q in enumerate(questions):
        print(f"\nQuestion {i + 1}: {q['question']}")
        for j, option in enumerate(q["options"]):
            print(f"{j + 1}. {option}")
        answer = input("Your answer (1-4): ")
        if q["options"][int(answer) - 1] ==
q["answer"]:
            print("Correct!")
            score += 1
        else:
            print(f"Wrong! The correct answer was
{q['answer']}.")

    print(f"\nYou scored
{score}/{len(questions)}.")
    if score > high_score:
        high_score = score
```

```python
        print("Congratulations! This is your new
high score!")

    play_again = input("Do you want to play
again? (yes/no): ").lower()
    if play_again != "yes":
        print(f"Your highest score was:
{high_score}")
        break

quiz_game_with_scores()
```

Practice Sets by Topic
Challenges for Loops and Iteration

1. ## Challenge 1: Sum of Multiples
   - Find the sum of all multiples of 3 or 5 below 100.

   python
   Copy code
   ```python
   def sum_of_multiples(limit):
       total = 0
       for i in range(limit):
           if i % 3 == 0 or i % 5 == 0:
               total += i
       return total

   print(sum_of_multiples(100))  # Output: 2318
   ```

2. ## Challenge 2: Factorial of a Number
   - Write a program to calculate the factorial of a given number using a loop.

   python
   Copy code
   ```python
   def factorial(n):
       result = 1
       for i in range(1, n + 1):
           result *= i
       return result

   print(factorial(5))  # Output: 120
   ```

3. Challenge 3: Fibonacci Sequence
  - Generate the first 10 numbers of the Fibonacci sequence using a loop.

python
Copy code

```python
def fibonacci(n):
    sequence = [0, 1]
    for i in range(2, n):
        sequence.append(sequence[-1] + sequence[-2])
    return sequence

print(fibonacci(10))  # Output: [0, 1, 1, 2, 3, 5, 8, 13, 21, 34]
```

4. Challenge 4: Prime Numbers in a Range
  - Print all prime numbers between 1 and 50.

python
Copy code

```python
def is_prime(num):
    if num < 2:
        return False
    for i in range(2, int(num**0.5) + 1):
        if num % i == 0:
            return False
    return True

for n in range(1, 51):
    if is_prime(n):
```

```
    print(n, end=" ")  # Output: 2 3 5 7 11 13 17 19
23 29 31 37 41 43 47
```

Challenges for Strings

1. **Challenge 1: Reverse a String**
   - ○ Write a program to reverse a string without using built-in functions.

   python
   Copy code
   ```
   def reverse_string(s):
       reversed_s = ""
       for char in s:
           reversed_s = char + reversed_s
       return reversed_s

   print(reverse_string("hello"))  # Output: "olleh"
   ```

2. **Challenge 2: Count Vowels**
   - ○ Count the number of vowels in a string.

   python
   Copy code
   ```
   def count_vowels(s):
       vowels = "aeiou"
       count = 0
       for char in s.lower():
           if char in vowels:
               count += 1
       return count
   ```

```python
print(count_vowels("programming"))  # Output: 3
```

3. **Challenge 3: Check Palindrome**
   - Determine if a given string is a palindrome.

```python
python
Copy code
def is_palindrome(s):
    return s == s[::-1]

print(is_palindrome("radar"))  # Output: True
print(is_palindrome("hello"))  # Output: False
```

4. **Challenge 4: Most Frequent Character**
   - Find the most frequent character in a string.

```python
python
Copy code
def most_frequent_char(s):
    frequency = {}
    for char in s:
        frequency[char] = frequency.get(char, 0) + 1
    return max(frequency, key=frequency.get)

print(most_frequent_char("hello world"))  # Output:
"l"
```

Challenges for Data Structures

1. Lists

1. **Challenge 1: Remove Duplicates**
   - Remove duplicates from a list while maintaining the original order.

python
Copy code
```python
def remove_duplicates(lst):
    unique = []
    for item in lst:
        if item not in unique:
            unique.append(item)
    return unique

print(remove_duplicates([1, 2, 2, 3, 4, 4, 5]))  #
Output: [1, 2, 3, 4, 5]
```

2. **Challenge 2: Rotate List**
   - Rotate a list to the right by k positions.

python
Copy code
```python
def rotate_list(lst, k):
    k %= len(lst)
    return lst[-k:] + lst[:-k]

print(rotate_list([1, 2, 3, 4, 5], 2))  # Output: [4, 5, 1,
2, 3]
```

2. Dictionaries

1. **Challenge 1: Word Frequency Counter**

- o Count the frequency of each word in a given sentence.

python
Copy code
```python
def word_frequency(sentence):
    words = sentence.split()
    frequency = {}
    for word in words:
        frequency[word] = frequency.get(word, 0) + 1
    return frequency

print(word_frequency("the quick brown fox jumps over the lazy dog"))
# Output: {'the': 2, 'quick': 1, 'brown': 1, 'fox': 1, 'jumps': 1, 'over': 1, 'lazy': 1, 'dog': 1}
```

2. **Challenge 2: Invert a Dictionary**
   - o Invert the keys and values of a dictionary.

python
Copy code
```python
def invert_dict(d):
    return {value: key for key, value in d.items()}

print(invert_dict({"a": 1, "b": 2, "c": 3}))  # Output: {1: 'a', 2: 'b', 3: 'c'}
```

3. Sets

1. **Challenge 1: Intersection of Two Lists**

- o Find common elements between two lists using sets.

python
Copy code
```python
def common_elements(lst1, lst2):
    return list(set(lst1) & set(lst2))

print(common_elements([1, 2, 3, 4], [3, 4, 5, 6]))  #
Output: [3, 4]
```

2. **Challenge 2: Unique Elements**
   - o Find unique elements from two lists combined.

python
Copy code
```python
def unique_elements(lst1, lst2):
    return list(set(lst1) ^ set(lst2))

print(unique_elements([1, 2, 3], [3, 4, 5]))  #
Output: [1, 2, 4, 5]
```

Solutions
Detailed Explanations for Each Challenge

Here's an explanation for each type of challenge, with examples and tips for improving your solutions.

1. Challenges for Loops and Iteration

Sum of Multiples

- **Explanation**: The goal is to iterate through numbers below a limit and sum only those divisible by 3 or 5. Use the % operator to check divisibility.
- **Improvement Tip**: Use list comprehensions for concise code.

```python
Copy code
def sum_of_multiples(limit):
    return sum([i for i in range(limit) if i % 3 == 0 or
i % 5 == 0])
```

Factorial of a Number

- **Explanation**: Multiply all integers from 1 to n. Use a loop or recursion.
- **Improvement Tip**: Use the math library for built-in factorial calculation.

```python
Copy code
import math
print(math.factorial(5))  # Output: 120
```

Fibonacci Sequence

- **Explanation**: Generate a series where each number is the sum of the two preceding ones. Start with [0, 1].
- **Improvement Tip**: Use generators for efficient memory usage.

```python
Copy code
def fibonacci(n):
    a, b = 0, 1
    for _ in range(n):
        yield a
        a, b = b, a + b

print(list(fibonacci(10)))  # Output: [0, 1, 1, 2, 3, 5, 8, 13, 21, 34]
```

Prime Numbers in a Range

- **Explanation**: Check divisibility for each number in the range. Use the square root method to reduce computation.
- **Improvement Tip**: Use a sieve algorithm for finding primes in bulk.

```python
Copy code
def sieve_of_eratosthenes(limit):
    primes = [True] * (limit + 1)
    primes[0] = primes[1] = False
```

```python
    for i in range(2, int(limit**0.5) + 1):
        if primes[i]:
            for j in range(i * i, limit + 1, i):
                primes[j] = False
    return [i for i, is_prime in enumerate(primes) if is_prime]

print(sieve_of_eratosthenes(50))  # Output: [2, 3, 5, 7, 11, ...]
```

2. Challenges for Strings

Reverse a String

- **Explanation**: Reverse a string by iterating over its characters in reverse order.
- **Improvement Tip**: Use slicing for simplicity.

```python
python
Copy code
print("hello"[::-1])  # Output: "olleh"
```

Count Vowels

Explanation: Count occurrences of vowels (a, e, i, o, u) in a string.

- **Improvement Tip**: Use collections.Counter for quick character frequency analysis.

```python
python
Copy code
```

```python
from collections import Counter

def count_vowels(s):
    counter = Counter(s.lower())
    return sum(counter[v] for v in "aeiou")

print(count_vowels("programming"))  # Output: 3
```

Check Palindrome

- **Explanation**: A string is a palindrome if it reads the same forwards and backwards.
- **Improvement Tip**: Use slicing for comparison to avoid loops.

```python
python
Copy code
print("radar" == "radar"[::-1])  # Output: True
```

Most Frequent Character

- **Explanation**: Find the character with the highest frequency in the string.
- **Improvement Tip**: Use max with a lambda function.

```python
python
Copy code
def most_frequent_char(s):
    return max(s, key=s.count)

print(most_frequent_char("hello world"))  # Output:
"l"
```

3. Challenges for Data Structures

Lists

Remove Duplicates:

- **Explanation**: Remove duplicates while maintaining the order of the original list.
- **Improvement Tip**: Use a set for fast lookup and a loop for preserving order.

```python
Copy code
def remove_duplicates(lst):
    seen = set()
    return [x for x in lst if not (x in seen or seen.add(x))]

print(remove_duplicates([1, 2, 2, 3, 4, 4]))  # Output: [1, 2, 3, 4]
```

Rotate List:

- **Explanation**: Move the last k elements to the front.
- **Improvement Tip**: Use slicing for a one-liner solution.

```python
Copy code
def rotate_list(lst, k):
    k %= len(lst)
    return lst[-k:] + lst[:-k]
```

Dictionaries

Word Frequency Counter:

- **Explanation**: Count the occurrence of each word in a sentence.
- **Improvement Tip**: Use collections.Counter for simplicity.

```python
Copy code
from collections import Counter
sentence = "the quick brown fox jumps over the lazy dog"
print(Counter(sentence.split()))  # Output: {'the': 2, 'quick': 1, ...}
```

Invert a Dictionary:

- **Explanation**: Swap keys and values in a dictionary.
- **Improvement Tip**: Handle duplicate values by grouping them in a list.

```python
Copy code
def invert_dict(d):
    inverted = {}
    for key, value in d.items():
        inverted.setdefault(value, []).append(key)
    return inverted
```

```python
print(invert_dict({"a": 1, "b": 2, "c": 1}))  # Output:
{1: ['a', 'c'], 2: ['b']}
```

Sets

Intersection of Two Lists:

- **Explanation**: Find common elements between two lists using sets.
- **Improvement Tip**: Use the & operator for intersection.

```python
python
Copy code
print(list(set([1, 2, 3]) & set([2, 3, 4])))  # Output:
[2, 3]
```

Unique Elements:

- **Explanation**: Find elements that are unique to each list.
- **Improvement Tip**: Use the ^ operator for symmetric difference.

```python
python
Copy code
print(list(set([1, 2, 3]) ^ set([3, 4, 5])))  # Output: [1, 2, 4, 5]
```

Tips for Improving Solutions

1. **Understand Built-In Functions**:
   - Use Python's powerful built-in functions and libraries like math, collections, and itertools to simplify and optimize your code.
2. **Optimize for Performance**:
   - Replace nested loops with dictionary or set lookups for faster execution.
   - For example, checking membership in a set ($O(1)$) is faster than checking in a list ($O(n)$).
3. **Code Readability**:
   - Use descriptive variable names.
   - Add comments to explain complex logic.
4. **Refactor Using List/Dict Comprehensions**:
   - Simplify loops and conditions into concise one-liners when appropriate.
5. **Test Edge Cases**:
   - Test solutions with edge cases like empty inputs, large data sets, or boundary values to ensure reliability.
6. **Learn Pythonic Techniques**:
   - Use slicing, lambda functions, and the zip function to write idiomatic Python code.
7. **Profile and Benchmark**:
   - Use modules like timeit or cProfile to measure the performance of your code and optimize bottlenecks.

By consistently applying these tips, your solutions will become cleaner, faster, and more Pythonic.

40

Conclusion

Reflecting on Progress

Taking a moment to evaluate what you've learned and accomplished so far can help solidify your knowledge and guide you towards the next steps.

Core Python Concepts Mastered

1. **Basic Syntax and Data Types**:
   - Understanding integers, floats, strings, lists, tuples, dictionaries, and sets.
   - Using conditionals (if-else) and loops (for, while).
2. **Control Flow and Iteration**:
   - Writing loops for repetitive tasks.
   - Using break, continue, and nested loops effectively.
3. **Functions and Modularization**:
   - Creating reusable functions with arguments and return values.
   - Understanding scope and recursion.
4. **Basic Object-Oriented Programming (OOP)**:
   - Defining classes and objects.
   - Using instance and class attributes.
   - Implementing simple methods.
5. **Error Handling**:
   - Catching and managing exceptions using try-except blocks.
6. **Libraries and Modules**:

- o Using built-in libraries like math, random, and collections.
- o Importing and creating custom modules.
7. **Practical Applications**:
   - o Automating tasks like file handling.
   - o Writing small projects (e.g., calculators, games, and basic scripts).

Signs You're Ready for Intermediate Python

- You can read and understand moderately complex Python code.
- You can debug your own programs and understand error messages.
- You've built small projects or solved challenges involving loops, functions, and basic data structures.
- You're curious about how to make your programs faster, cleaner, and more powerful.

Moving to Intermediate Python Concepts

1. Advanced Python Syntax

- **List, Dictionary, and Set Comprehensions**:
  - o Create concise and efficient one-liners for generating lists or dictionaries.

```python
Copy code
numbers = [x**2 for x in range(10) if x % 2 == 0]
print(numbers)  # Output: [0, 4, 16, 36, 64]
```

- **Unpacking and Star Expressions**:
  - Use unpacking for cleaner code.

```python
Copy code
a, *b, c = [1, 2, 3, 4, 5]
print(a, b, c)  # Output: 1 [2, 3, 4] 5
```

2. Advanced Data Structures

- **Collections Module**:
  - Explore specialized data types like defaultdict, Counter, and deque.

```python
Copy code
from collections import Counter
print(Counter("mississippi"))  # Output:
Counter({'i': 4, 's': 4, 'p': 2, 'm': 1})
```

- **Custom Classes and Advanced OOP**:
  - Learn inheritance, polymorphism, and method overriding.

```python
Copy code
class Animal:
    def speak(self):
        pass

class Dog(Animal):
    def speak(self):
```

```python
    return "Woof!"

print(Dog().speak())  # Output: "Woof!"
```

3. File Handling and Automation

- **Context Managers**:
    - Use with statements for cleaner and safer file handling.

    python
    Copy code
    ```python
    with open("example.txt", "r") as file:
        content = file.read()
    ```

- **Automation**:
    - Automate repetitive tasks using scripts. Examples include renaming files or scraping data from websites using BeautifulSoup.

4. Algorithms and Problem Solving

- **Sorting and Searching**:
    - Implement algorithms like quicksort, mergesort, and binary search.
- **Dynamic Programming**:
    - Solve optimization problems with memoization and recursion.

5. Asynchronous Programming

- Learn to work with concurrent tasks using asyncio, threads, and processes.

python
Copy code
```python
import asyncio

async def say_hello():
    print("Hello")
    await asyncio.sleep(1)
    print("World")

asyncio.run(say_hello())
```

6. Performance Optimization

- **Profiling and Debugging**:
  - Use cProfile and timeit to identify bottlenecks.
- **Generators**:
  - Replace lists with generators for memory efficiency.

python
Copy code
```python
def generate_numbers():
    for i in range(10):
        yield i
print(list(generate_numbers()))  # Output: [0, 1, 2, ..., 9]
```

7. Testing and Debugging

- Write tests using unittest or pytest.
- Learn logging to monitor your applications.

8. Web Development

- **Django**:
    - Build web applications with robust backends.
- **Flask**:
    - Create lightweight APIs or apps for specific purposes.

9. Python for Data Science

- **Data Libraries**:
    - Learn pandas for data manipulation and NumPy for numerical computation.
- **Visualization**:
    - Use Matplotlib and Seaborn for creating insightful visualizations.

10. APIs and Integration

- Learn how to consume and build REST APIs.

```python
Copy code
import requests

response = requests.get("https://api.example.com/data")
```

```
print(response.json())
```

Tips for Transitioning

1. **Work on Intermediate-Level Projects**:
   - Build a personal budget tracker.
   - Create a to-do list with a database backend using SQLite.
2. **Solve Algorithmic Challenges**:
   - Use platforms like **LeetCode, HackerRank,** or **Codewars** to practice.
   - Aim for problems tagged as "medium."
3. **Collaborate on Open Source**:
   - Contribute to GitHub projects to gain real-world coding experience.
4. **Learn Version Control**:
   - Master Git and GitHub for collaborative development.
5. **Join Python Communities**:
   - Engage with forums like Reddit's **r/Python**, Python Discord, or local Python meetups.

Roadmap Summary

Focus Area	Key Activities
Advanced Syntax	List comprehensions, unpacking, custom iterators.
OOP and Design	Implement inheritance,

Focus Area	Key Activities
Patterns	polymorphism, and singleton.
Data Structures	Use collections and create efficient algorithms.
Web Development	Build apps using Django or Flask.
Data Science	Work with pandas, NumPy, and matplotlib.
Performance Optimization	Use generators, profiling, and multithreading.
Testing	Write unit tests using unittest or pytest